Debt is Slavery

Get Out of Debt, Gain Control Of Your Finances, and Reclaim Your Freedom and Your Life!

FIRST EDITION

Debt is Slavery

and **9** Other Things I Wish My Dad Had Taught Me About Money

MICHAEL MIHALIK

OCTOBER MIST
PUBLISHING

Seattle, Washington

Debt is Slavery

and 9 Other Things I Wish My Dad Had Taught Me About Money

BY MICHAEL MIHALIK

Copyright © 2007 by Michael Thomas Mihalik

Published by:

October Mist Publishing   SAN: 850–959X
PO Box 70809   orders@OctoberMist.com
Seattle, WA 98127   http://www.OctoberMist.com

ISBN-10, print ed. 0-9785457-0-2
ISBN-13, print ed. 978-0-9785457-0-3

First Printing 2007

Book Design: Peri Poloni-Gabriel, Knockout Design, www.knockoutbooks.com

Library of Congress Control Number: 2006926841

——————— Publisher's Cataloging-in-Publication ———————
(Provided by Quality Books, Inc.)

Mihalik, Michael.
   Debt is slavery : and 9 other things I wish my dad had taught me about money / by Michael Mihalik. — 1st ed.
   p. cm.
   "Get out of debt, gain control of your finances, and reclaim your freedom and your life!"
   LCCN 2006926841
   ISBN-13: 978-0-9785457-0-3
   ISBN-10: 0-9785457-0-2

   1. Finance, Personal. 2. Debt. 3. Consumer credit.
I. Title.

HG179.M57 2007   332.024'02
                                     QBI06-600324

To my father.

Table of Contents

—ɯ—

Disclaimer   **10**

Acknowledgments   **11**

Introduction   **13**

How to Choose a Teacher 14
   So How Do I Rate? 14
Money 18
   Times Have Changed 19
   A Quick History of Money 20
   Why Money Has Value 21
   Our Relationship With Money 22

CHAPTER 1: **Debt is Slavery**   **23**

The Nature of Debt 24
The Two Kinds of Debt 25
Credit Card Debt 27
Why Do We Go into Debt? 28
Is There "Good Debt"? 28
You Don't Own It if You Owe Money on It 29
Mortgages 30
Tapping Your Home Equity 30
Conclusion 34

CHAPTER 2: **Time May Not Be Money, But Money
Definitely Is Time**   **35**

Money vs. Time 36
So What Should We Do? 37

CHAPTER 3: **Possessions are a Prison** 39

The Hidden Cost of Possessions 40

The Giant Marketing Machine 43

Put Stuff Back into Circulation 45

Accomplish and Achieve, Don't Accumulate 47

Rules to Control the Stuff in Your Life 48

Conclusion 52

CHAPTER 4: **Be Aware of the Ongoing Campaign to Separate You From Your Money** 53

Status/Fashion 55

Conclusion 57

CHAPTER 5: **Money Buys Freedom** 59

Retirement 61

Conclusion 62

CHAPTER 6: **Don't Sell Your Soul for a Salary** 63

How Many People Like Their Jobs? 64

How We Choose Our Careers 64

So How Should We Choose Our Jobs? 67

Other Considerations 68

Conclusion 69

CHAPTER 7: **Own** 71

Income-Producing Assets vs. Income-Consuming Assets 72

Financial Windfalls 74

How to Earn Money Without Spending Time 75

Stocks 75

Possibly the Worst Way You Can Spend Your Money 76

The Best Way to Buy a Car 77

Conclusion 78

CHAPTER 8: **Spend Less Than You Earn By Controlling Your Expenses**   **79**

The Two Different Kinds of Expenses 79

Raises. 81

Controlling Your Expenses Has a Wonderful Effect on
    Your Savings. 81

Minimizing Your Monthly Bills 82

Conclusion. 83

CHAPTER 9: **Save 50 Percent of Your Salary**   **85**

CHAPTER 10: **Control Your Money or Your Money Will Control You (How to Plan Your Finances)**   **89**

Planning Your Finances Leads to Financial Security 90

Eliminating Debt 91

Creating Your Financial Plan 92

    Step 1: Collect the Necessary Tools. 93

    Step 2: Figure Out How Much Money You Make. 94

    Step 3: Figure Out How Much Money You Owe 95

    Step 4: List Your Monthly Bills. 96

    Step 5: Create a Paycheck-by-Paycheck Financial Plan 98

Minimizing Your Expenses. 102

Starting Your Debt-Elimination Plan 103

Paying Off Credit Card Debt 104

Unexpected or Unusual Expenses. 108

Create a False Sense of Scarcity 109

Conclusion. 110

CHAPTER 11: **A Bonus**   **111**

Appendix   **115**

About the Author   **123**

—Ⱳ—

Disclaimer

—◠◡◠—

This book contains the opinions and ideas of its author. It is based on the author's personal experiences and describes the methods he used to regain control of his finances after accumulating a large amount of debt.

This book is not meant to provide investment or legal advice. The author and the publisher do not provide financial, legal, or other professional services. Anyone seeking advice on these subjects should consult licensed professionals.

Every effort has been made to ensure that the information contained in this book is accurate. However, as with any human endeavor, mistakes may have been made. It is prudent for the reader to not rely solely upon this book, but to use it as a guide. Also, information is up-to-date only as of the publication of this book.

The author and the publisher shall not have either liability or responsibility to any person or entity with respect to any loss or damage caused, or alleged to have been caused, directly or indirectly, by the information contained in this book.

If you do not agree with, or do not wish to be bound by, the above, please return this book to the publisher immediately for a full refund.

—◠◡◠—

Acknowledgments

—⁓—

This book would not have been possible without the help and support of many people.

The wonderful cover and interior for this book were created by Peri Poloni-Gabriel of Knockout Design. My thanks also go to Monica Thomas of Knockout Design for her hard work and patience.

My deepest gratitude goes to my editors, Heidi Thomas, of SunCatcher Publications, and Leslie Kooy, and to the Doors for allowing me to quote lyrics from one of their timeless songs.

I'd also like to express my appreciation to my group of "first readers": Beverly Molloy, Rick Nagel, Steve Brooks, Mark Roberts, Poppy Roberts, Jerry Newman, and Loraine Migliori. Your suggestions and comments improved my book tremendously.

Thank you, Abby, for your enthusiastic embrace of my money philosophy, which gave me the idea to write this book.

Beverly, thanks for believing in me.

Thank you, Mom, for the sacrifices you made to raise me and Loraine after Dad's death.

And finally, thanks, Dad, for all the lessons you taught me in the 13 years we had together.

—⁓—

Introduction

—〰—

From our Founding Fathers to Ward Cleaver, fathers are universally seen as sources of wisdom. We seek guidance and advice from our fathers, hoping to tap into their life experience and knowledge.

My father died when I was 13 years old. Since then, I've often wished I had a father or father figure to turn to for advice. I've sought mentors to take my father's place, but, unfortunately, good mentors—willing mentors—are hard to find.

I've had to come up with my own rules as I've slogged through life. That's not the easiest way to learn. I wish someone had just taught me the rules, but fate had other plans for me.

As part of my quest for knowledge, I have read many "self-help" books. Some were useful, others not. A common attribute of many "self-help" books is they are too long. These books could easily be half as long and twice as effective and interesting. With this in mind, I have tried to keep this book short and to-the-point.

If you never seem to have enough money, if you're drowning in debt, if it seems like you'll never get ahead financially, or if you're forced to work at a job you dislike just to pay the bills, this book has something for you.

The lessons in this book have been learned through hard experience—my hard experience. I will often illustrate a point with an example from my life. We all learn best through experience. However, it's easier, quicker, and less painful to learn from someone else's experience than to muddle through on our own.

This book describes a new way of thinking. It can change your life.

How to Choose a Teacher

I have learned that before you take anyone's advice, you should evaluate them by the following criteria:

1) *Have they done what they are teaching?*

If you wanted to learn how to play basketball, who would you rather ask: Michael Jordan or your grandmother? Even if your grandmother played basketball in her youth, I think you'd rather ask Michael for his advice.

If you want to learn something, learn from someone who has done what they are teaching.

2) *Do they have your best interests at heart?*

If someone is teaching you about insurance so they can sell you a policy, you would be wise to question what they are telling you. They may be thinking about their commission and not what's best for you.

So How Do I Rate?

I believe you should apply these same criteria to me.

1) *Have I done what I am teaching?*

I received my first "pre-approved" credit card when I was a senior in high school. I was ecstatic. A credit card—I was grown-up now! I signed the application, mailed it back, and when I received the card three weeks later, I was off to the store. I spent $200 on Calvin Klein polo shirts and Nike shoes.

That was the beginning of a long, painful ride.

After graduating from high school, I received a full-ride academic scholarship to the University of Washington.

Although I didn't have much money, I resolved not to miss out on any of the fun during college. I worked part-time, which provided some income, but not enough.

I used credit cards to make up the difference. They were easy to get and I got a bunch. I figured that with the "huge" salary I'd earn after graduation, I would easily pay off my college credit card debt.

I used credit cards to buy CDs, a racing bike, skis, stereo equipment, clothes, dinner for my dates, concert tickets, airplane tickets, and ski trips.

I didn't keep track of the amount of debt, because I planned to pay it off quickly once I graduated and started making the "big bucks."

Well, it didn't exactly work out that way.

After graduating with a degree in Mechanical Engineering, I started my first "real job." I was making $28,500 per year and thought it would be difficult to spend it all. I quickly forgot my pledge to use my new-found wealth to pay off my college debt. I moved into a house with some friends and bought a more expensive car. I lived the high life—ski trips to Canada and Oregon, road trips, concerts, movies, and expensive dinners to impress the girls.

Suddenly, my paychecks weren't lasting as long as they used to. I started to run out of money halfway between checks. I couldn't make more than the minimum payments on my credit cards. Whenever I had some money left over, I would receive an unexpected or forgotten bill, which would quickly wipe out the surplus.

I stopped having fun. I couldn't wait until the next payday.

I was in trouble.

I finally gathered the courage to do something I had been avoiding for months. I sat down with a stack of credit card statements, bank statements, and bills and added up my debt.

I owed:

- ➤ $10,000 on 10 credit cards
- ➤ $13,000 on a car loan
- ➤ $2,500 in student loans
- ➤ $535 on a medical bill
- ➤ $1,500 on a loan for an electronic keyboard

On top of that, my monthly bills included $300 in rent and $100 in car insurance. Then there were utilities, gas, food, and other expenses.

Needless to say, I didn't have much money left over for fun.

I was 24 years old and felt like I was trapped in a dark box that was shrinking around me. I often woke up in the middle of the night in a panic, worried about my future. My enjoyment of life diminished.

Personal debt can cause so much anxiety that it actually affects your physical health. I developed an ulcer and heart palpitations.

I began to despair because I saw no chance of paying off my debt before I was 40. I thought about filing for bankruptcy, but who wants to be bankrupt at the age of 24?

I had to come up with a plan.

The first thing I did was admit that it was my fault I had a paralyzing amount of debt. I had created this situation for myself. I realized debt was ruining my life and decided to pay it off as quickly as possible.

After some trial and error, I created and implemented a debt-elimination plan. I designed a way to plan my finances, made some tough sacrifices, worked a lot of overtime, and paid off most of my debt (except the car loan) in a little over a year.

After that hellish year, I resolved never to put myself in that situation again. I decided to live within my means. That painful year forced me to create a philosophy about money that has since served me well.

Since then, I have experienced two periods of career and financial hardship, but I survived them both—thanks to my philosophy about money.

So, yes, I have done what I am teaching.

Besides, I'm writing the first draft of this book during a six-week hiatus from work—without pay. I'm able to take the time off because I have been successful at managing my money and planning my finances.

2) *Do I have your best interests at heart?*

When I decided to get out of debt and improve my relationship with money, I realized I'd need some advice. Since my father wasn't around, I looked for a book that could help me. I wanted a short, easy-to-read book that would give me a straightforward and practical method for getting rid of my debt. I found some books, but they were too long. I don't have an aversion to long books, but I wanted to get started right away. I didn't want to waste time reading a 300-page book. Besides, it seemed many of those 300 pages were spent trying to sell the author's other books and products.

After I eliminated my debt and gained control of my finances, I wanted to help other people do the same, so I decided to write the book I wish had been available to me.

I am not selling anything beyond this book. The only things you need to implement my money philosophy are the desire to change, this book, and a few inexpensive tools you can buy at any local drugstore.

I have two main goals for this book:

➤ To change the way you think about money.

All the techniques and methods in the world won't help if you don't change the way you *think* about money.

➤ To give you concrete methods to control your finances.

I want to help you eliminate debt and live a happy, prosperous financial life—and to get you started as soon as possible. I want you to have a healthy relationship with money and gain control of your finances and your life. I want you to benefit from my experience, so you can avoid the pain I experienced as I dealt with my paralyzing debt.

But most of all, I want you to pass these lessons on to your children, so they won't ever have to say, "I wish my parents had taught me that."

Money

Why did I choose to write a book about money? Aren't we taught that money really isn't that important and "the love of money is the root of all evil?" Isn't it shallow to think too much about money? Why didn't I instead write a book about peace, love, and understanding?

Like it or not, we need money to live in our society. We use money to provide the basic necessities of life: food, clothing, and shelter. Money also provides us with luxuries and comforts. It influences almost every aspect of our lives.

Money determines:

➤ How we spend our time.

➤ What neighborhood we live in.

➤ What kind of house we own or whether we even own a house.

➤ What kind of car we drive.

➤ Where we go on vacation.

➤ Who we hang out with.

➤ Whether we can retire.

➤ Which schools we or our children can attend.

➤ How much free time we have.

➤ What hobbies we have.

➤ How much we can help others in need.

➤ Our peace of mind.

I've had people tell me "Money just isn't important to me." Yet those same people spend eight or more hours a day going to jobs they hate. From Monday to Friday, one-third of their lives is spent earning money, and yet they say "money just isn't that important to me." If money isn't so important, why do they spend the best hours of the day earning money?

What they do speaks so loudly I can hardly hear what they say.

How much money we have determines a large part of the daily reality of our lives and yet, most of us were never taught even basic lessons about money.

I hope to remedy that with this book. I want to change your relationship with money. I want to change the way you think about money. I want you to use money to gain more freedom and happiness in your life.

Times Have Changed

Our economy has evolved from being local to global. People are being laid off as their jobs either become obsolete or are sent to another country. The evolution of technology and the Internet has made it possible to send customer service, factory, computer programming, and engineering jobs overseas where foreign workers can be hired for pennies on the dollar.

American workers used to work their entire career at one company and retire comfortably with company-provided pensions. Companies provided free health insurance and other benefits for their employees.

That time is past. We can no longer count on our employers to provide for our financial security. We also can no longer rely on government programs such as Social Security to provide us with retirement income.

More than ever, we need to gain control of our own financial futures.

A Quick History of Money

Early economies were based on bartering. There was no money; people traded goods and services. For example, I might trade a chicken, two goats, and a day's labor in your fields in exchange for your cow.

Since chickens, goats, and cows don't fit neatly into pockets, wallets, or purses, coins were invented. At first, coins were made of precious metals such as gold and silver. As demand for money increased, coins were made from more common metals such as bronze (an alloy of copper and tin).

The governments that issued the coins decreed they were "legal tender," which meant that they could be used to pay debts and to purchase goods and services. People started using coins because they were easy to carry and limited in supply.

From that point on, economies depended on money instead of bartering to operate. As civilizations and technology improved, money progressed from metal coins to paper money, then to the "virtual" money we have today. The majority of money today is not physical, but resides as data on a computer somewhere.

Why Money Has Value

So what gives money its value?

As we've learned, coins were originally made of precious materials such as silver and gold. These coins were valuable because they were made of valuable material. Eventually, there wasn't enough silver and gold to support the growth of the currency, so new coins were made of inexpensive metals such as bronze, nickel, and copper.

It soon became apparent that coins were too bulky and heavy to carry around for expensive purchases, so paper money was invented. For years, paper money had value because it was directly supported by silver or gold. The U.S. dollar was exchangeable for gold until 1971, when President Richard Nixon took the dollar off the "gold standard."

Even coins are no longer made of valuable metals. A modern quarter is made of 91.67 percent copper and 8.33 percent nickel. It weighs about 5.7 grams or 0.2 ounces. Copper currently sells for about $2.15 per pound. So a quarter contains about three cents worth of copper, yet, a quarter is valued at 25 cents.

Similarly, bills are nothing but intricately printed pieces of paper, with no value in and of themselves. Yet, we accept paper money as payment for goods and services.

Why?

Money has value because it is limited in supply and the issuing government mandates by law that it has value and will be accepted for payments of debt and for goods and services.

Say what? Money has value because the government says it has value?

Yes. Money's value is in its symbolic worth, which is supported by the full faith and support of the issuing government. It sounds sort of hokey, but that's the way the system works today.

However it derives its value, money is a powerful tool. If used properly, it can help us on the road to freedom, opportunity, and happiness.

Our Relationship With Money

It is easy to obsess about money, especially if you don't have any. Most people do not have a good relationship with money. They have never taken the time to figure out how to use money to provide not only the three essentials of life, but also freedom and opportunity, which are the true keys to happiness.

Since there are many books out there that deal with the mechanics of money (how to invest in real estate, how to choose mutual funds, how to plan for retirement), I'm not going to spend a lot of time talking about those topics. Instead, I'm going to focus on changing the way you *think* about money. I will also describe in detail a method for planning your finances and getting out of debt. (For readers who have questions about financial terms and concepts that I use in this book, please see the Appendix.)

The ideas in this book can apply to everybody—young, old or in-between, single or married, kids or no kids. This book talks about *truth*, and truth does not change based on marital status, age, or family size.

By changing the way we think about money and avoiding common traps and misconceptions, we can reach the point where we control our money instead of letting it control us.

I have learned, from hard experience, some lessons about money. This book focuses on 10 of those lessons.

Let's get started!

—⚏—

Debt is Slavery

—ᴍ—

Debt is slavery.

That sure sounds like an extreme statement, but just because it sounds extreme doesn't mean it isn't true.

> **Slavery:** *The state of being bound in servitude as an instrument of labor.*

Do you ever wake up in the morning and groan "I don't want to go to work today?"

As you lie in bed toying with the idea of staying home, your thoughts turn to all the bills you have to pay: the mortgage, car payment, credit card bills, tuition, insurance premiums, electricity, phone, cable, groceries...

So you drag your tired self out of your warm bed, drink a pot of coffee, and drive to work (in your cool car—only 43 more payments and that baby is all yours!)

You drag yourself out of bed and go to work, because you *have* to.

Isn't that a form of slavery?

If you didn't have all of those financial obligations, if you had enough money in the bank, wouldn't you rather take the day off and enjoy life? You would rather take the day off, but you go to work because *debt is a cruel master*. If you owe others money, they have power over you.

The sad part is, many of us willingly put ourselves into this slavery by taking on debt.

We have the power to control our money and our lives. We hold the key to unlock the chains that bind us. Yet we either choose not to or we don't know how.

The Nature of Debt

Debt. It's easy to get and everyone seems to have it: mortgages, car loans, student loans, and those evil little pieces of plastic—CREDIT CARDS! We like credit cards so much that one isn't enough. We have credit cards from VISA, MasterCard, Nordstrom, Chevron, Target, and Sears. We can have regular cards or gold cards. If gold isn't good enough, we can upgrade to platinum. We use credit cards to buy groceries, expensive vacations, and everything in between.

> **Debt:** An obligation or liability to pay something to another person.

There are many kinds of debt:
- ➤ Home mortgages
- ➤ Credit cards
- ➤ Car loans
- ➤ Boat loans
- ➤ RV loans
- ➤ Motorcycle loans
- ➤ Consumer loans
- ➤ Lines of credit
- ➤ Home equity loans
- ➤ Payday loans
- ➤ Student loans

We use debt to go on buying binges and then moan and groan when the bills come. It can be an endless cycle and a painful one. We accumulate more and more debt until we feel like we're suffocating.

We accumulate debt because we don't have enough cash to make a purchase. When we borrow money, we are spending our future earnings. If we can't pay for it today, why do we think we can pay for it tomorrow? We are spending money we don't have or haven't yet earned to buy something now.

Yeah, I know, some people justify using certain credit cards because they earn "points" or "miles." That's fine. If you have the discipline and the means to pay off your credit card every month, then go right ahead and earn those free flights. But you're in the minority. Most of us aren't that disciplined.

And sure, lately, people have been taking on staggering amounts of debt to buy real estate. They have been making lots of money. That's a great idea—while it works.

But *debt is slavery*. I'm not saying we should all live like monks, but we definitely should control how much money we borrow.

Too many people hate their jobs but are afraid to leave, because they wouldn't be able to pay their mortgage, credit card bills, car loans, or boat loans. Debt can turn a free, happy person into a bitter human being. Debt can turn you into a slave.

The Two Kinds of Debt

There are two kinds of debt:

➤ Secured Debt

➤ Unsecured Debt

Secured Debt

Secured debt is when you borrow money to buy a specific asset. The asset provides collateral to the lender. The lender legally owns the asset until you pay it off. If you don't make your payments, the lender can repossess the asset, sell it, and keep the money.

> **Collateral:** *Property acceptable as security for a loan or other obligation.*

Examples of secured debt are car loans, boat loans, RV loans, and home mortgages.

Do you have a car loan? If so, look at your car registration. The registration will list two owners: the "registered owner" and the "legal owner." If you still owe money on your car, you are the "registered owner," but the lender is the "legal owner." The lender remains the "legal owner" until you pay off the loan.

Even if you have paid off 90 percent of the loan, if you fail to make your payments, the lender will repossess your car, sell it, and keep all of the proceeds.

Secured debt is "safer" than unsecured debt because, if you get into trouble, you can always sell the asset to pay off the loan. The danger is that the asset may not be worth enough to cover the amount still owed on it.

EXAMPLE

You owe $5,000 on your car, but your car is only worth $4,000. Even if you sell the car, you have to come up with another $1,000 to pay off the loan.

Debt is slavery.

Unsecured Debt

Unsecured debt is when you borrow money with no collateral provided to the lender.

Two examples of unsecured debt are credit cards and lines of credit.

When you have a credit card, you can buy anything. If you don't make the payments, the lender will not repossess the clothes, the stereo, or the trip to Maui. However, they still have legal power over you and can make your life miserable. Creditors can take you to court, put liens on your assets, and garnish your wages.

Unsecured debt is dangerous. You can spend a lot of money buying things that have no lasting value, such as dining out and vacations. Once you eat your dinner or go on your trip, they have zero value, yet you still have to pay back the money you borrowed to purchase them.

If you run into trouble with your unsecured debt, there's very little you can sell to pay off the debt. Clothing is worthless once you wear it and wash it. Shoes are the same. Electronic items hold some value, but become obsolete so quickly that they soon become worthless as well.

Credit Card Debt

How many of you are still paying for:

➤ The vacation you took last summer?

➤ The elegant, romantic Valentine's Day dinner from last February?

➤ The pair of expensive, Italian shoes you gave to Goodwill last Saturday?

➤ Christmas presents your kids no longer play with?

➤ Top-of-the-line electronic gear that's now obsolete?

People often use credit cards to buy things with no lasting value. For example, people use credit cards to buy dinner, which is immediately eaten, and then it's gone. But the payments remain. Months after we've eaten the dinner, we may still be paying for it.

Does that make sense? Do you even know which past purchases your monthly credit card payments are paying for?

Can you remember the last time your credit card balance was zero? Do you always have a balance on your credit cards? If so, you're paying for stuff today that may have long ago disappeared from your life.

Using a credit card is *borrowing money* and borrowing money can make you a debt slave.

Debt is slavery.

Why Do We Go Into Debt?

People go into debt for many reasons, including:

➤ Impulsive buying.

➤ "Rewarding" themselves.

➤ Keeping up with the Joneses.

➤ Impressing other people.

➤ Overcoming depression or a feeling of inadequacy.

We could probably summarize why people go into debt with this one statement:

➤ People go into debt because they want to live a lifestyle beyond what they can afford.

Is There "Good Debt?"

Can there be "good debt?"

Debt can be "good" if it is used to buy something that will produce value and/or income in the future.

For example, borrowing money to pay for a college education can be "good debt." A college education can produce value and income in the future.

Another example of "good debt" is borrowing money to start a business. A business can produce value and income in the future. The income can then be used to pay off the debt.

A third example of "good debt" is borrowing money to make a large purchase such as a house. (People rarely have enough money to purchase a house for cash.) However, there is a caveat that comes with this kind of debt. We must make sure that we are getting value for our money. If we overpay or overextend our finances for a house, a mortgage is not "good debt."

Borrowing money to buy a car is not "good debt", but is sometimes necessary. Few of us have the money to pay cash for a car, so I'll call a car loan "acceptable debt".

However, cars usually decrease in value at a faster rate than the loan is being paid off. (The same applies to boats, motorcycles, and RVs.) It's easy to get "upside down" on a car loan—where you owe more on a car than it is worth.

You Don't Own It if You Owe Money On It

People who take out a mortgage to buy a house are proud to call themselves "homeowners." But is that accurate?

> **Equity:** The monetary value of an asset beyond the amount owed on that asset.

Do you really "own" your house? If you have a house that's worth $200,000 and you have $40,000 in equity, doesn't the bank own 80 percent while you own 20 percent? If you stopped paying your mortgage, what would happen? Would the bank pay you $40,000 to buy your part of the house?

Of course not. That's because as long as you owe money on your house, you don't truly own the house—the bank does. If you stop paying your mortgage, the bank will repossess the house, evict you, sell the house, and pay you nothing.

The same thing applies to your car, your boat, and your vacation home on the coast. If you owe money on it, *you don't own it.*

> **EXAMPLE**
>
> Your house is worth $200,000. You owe $160,000 on the mortgage.
>
> Your equity (your portion of the house's value) is:
> $200,000 – $160,000 = **$40,000**

Mortgages

Am I saying that we shouldn't have mortgages, that we shouldn't buy houses?

Of course not, but I want to change the way you look at debt. *Mortgages are debt.*

The word "mortgage" is derived from the Latin word "mort," which means "death," and the Germanic word "gage," which means "pledge." So "mortgage" means "death pledge." What does that tell you?

Borrowing money to buy a house can be categorized as "good debt," but you should still focus on paying it off as soon as possible. Don't fall for the advertisements to "extract your equity" by refinancing or taking out a home equity loan. Pay off your mortgage as soon as possible.

Debt—in all its forms—is slavery.

Tapping Your Home Equity

Lately, low interest rates and rising property values have encouraged people to extract their home equity by refinancing their mortgages. People often use this extracted equity to "consolidate their debt," using the extra money to pay off credit card bills, auto loans, student loans, etc.

Justifications for this action includes:

➤ The interest rate will be lower.

➤ The interest is now tax deductible.

➤ The monthly payments go down.

Let's analyze this reasoning with the following example:

EXAMPLE
Bob refinances his mortgage and extracts cash (equity) to buy a new car.

The Original Purchase

House Value	$120,000.00
Down Payment	$15,000.00
Loan Balance	$105,000.00
Interest Rate	8.00%
Length of Loan	30 years
Monthly Payment	$770.00

1) Bob bought his house five years ago for $120,000.

2) He put $15,000 down and took out a mortgage for the balance ($105,000).

3) The original mortgage was a 30-year fixed-rate at 8 percent. The monthly payments are $770.

The Refinanced Mortgage

House Value	$200,000.00
Loan Balance (after taking out $20,000)	$120,000.00
Interest Rate	6.00%
Length of Loan	30 years
Monthly Payment	$719.00

(Continues on next page)

(Continued from previous page)

1) Five years later, Bob's house is worth $200,000. Because he's been paying down the balance, he now owes $100,000. He has $100,000 in equity ($200,000 minus $100,000).

2) Bob refinances his house, using a 30-year fixed-rate mortgage at 6 percent.

3) Bob does a "cash-out" refinance, which means he will extract $20,000 of his equity. He gets a check for $20,000 at closing.

4) Bob's new mortgage balance is $120,000 and the new monthly payment is $719. Bob just got $20,000 in "free" money and his payments went down $51 a month ($770 minus $719).

5) Bob's equity is now $80,000 ($200,000 minus $120,000).

6) Bob uses the $20,000 of "extracted equity" to pay cash for a new car.

What a bargain! Bob lowered his monthly payments by $51 a month and got a "free" car in the process.

But What Really Happened?

	Original Loan at the Time of Refinancing	Refinanced Loan	
House Value	$200,000.00	$200,000.00	
Loan Balance	$100,000.00	$120,000.00	
Bob's Equity	$100,000.00	$80,000.00	
Interest Rate	8.00%	6.00%	
Time Left on Loan	25 years	30 years	
Monthly Payment	$770.00	$719.00	

Comparison of Bob's Original Mortgage
with the Refinanced Mortgage

1) Bob increased his mortgage balance (his debt) by $20,000.

2) He used that $20,000 to buy a new car.

(Continues on next page)

(Continued from previous page)

3) The extra $20,000 in debt is now amortized over 30 years.

4) A standard car loan is amortized over 2 to 6 years

5) Bob just took out a 30-year car loan!

6) It is unlikely Bob will keep the car for more than 10 years.

7) Bob will be making payments on his "new" car for 20 years after he gets rid of it.

8) Not only that, but Bob had 25 years left on the old mortgage. Now that he's refinanced, he has **30** years left on the new one. He just added another 5 years to the length of the loan.

Did Bob make a good financial decision?

Of course not. But people do things like this all the time.

Bob was right to refinance his 8-percent mortgage into a 6-percent mortgage, but he shouldn't have taken out $20,000 to buy a car.

If Bob had just refinanced his 8-percent mortgage at 6-percent, and not added $20,000 to the loan balance, his payment would have dropped from $770 to $599.

He would have increased his payment period from 25 years to 30 years, but his payment would have fallen $171 a month!

	Original Loan (at the time of refinancing)	Refinanced Loan	
House Value	$200,000.00	$200,000.00	
Loan Balance	$100,000.00	$100,000.00	⇐
Bob's Equity	$100,000.00	$100,000.00	
Interest Rate	8.00%	6.00%	
Monthly Payment	$770.00	$599.00	⇐
Time Left on Loan	25 years	30 years	

Instead, Bob has taken out a 30-year car loan. By the time the mortgage is paid off, Bob will have paid $43,167.72 for his car, long after the car has been sent to the junkyard.

> **Amortize:** To liquidate a debt by installment payments. To "amortize" a loan over 30 years means calculating payments based on a 30-year payoff period.

But interest on a car loan isn't tax-deductible and the interest on Bob's mortgage is, right?

That's true. But let's analyze what "tax-deductible" means. Tax-deductions work like this:

1) You spend $1,000 in mortgage interest.

2) You write that off against your income.

3) If you're in the 28 percent tax bracket, you save $280 in taxes.

What a bargain! You just spent $1,000 in interest to get back $280. You received nothing of tangible value for the $1,000—it was a "fee" for borrowing money to buy the house. Yet, somehow spending $1,000 and getting $280 in return is supposed to be a good deal.

If you think that's a good deal, I'd be more than happy to give you a better one—if you give me $1,000, I'll gladly give you back $300!

When I put it like that, it doesn't sound that great, does it?

It's even worse when you consider that people refinance their mortgages, "extract" their home equity, and use the money to pay off credit card debt.

These people are stretching out their credit card payments for 30 years. For the next 30 years, they will be making payments on that steak dinner they had last Friday, those socks they bought at Macy's, and the trendy electronic gadget that will be obsolete in six months.

Conclusion

The next time you pull out your credit card to buy something, or are tempted to borrow money, remember: *Debt is Slavery.*

—⁓—

CHAPTER 2

Time May Not Be Money, But Money Definitely Is Time

—⚋—

One of my favorite song lyrics is from the Doors song, "Five to One":

"Trading your hours for a handful of dimes."

That single line hits upon a great truth of American life—most of us trade our time, our *lives,* for money. We spend the best hours of the best days of the best years of our lives working at a job we often don't even like. Every week, we trade 40 or more hours of our lives for "a handful of dimes".

Why?

We go to work to make money to buy stuff we don't need and don't use, or to pay back the debt we accumulated buying things we don't need and don't use.

A while ago, I came up with what I thought was a unique way of looking at money. When I mentioned it to my friends, they thought I was nuts.

Every time I wanted to spend money, I'd think of that money as time. For example, if I made $12 an hour and wanted to buy a $12 CD, I'd say that the CD cost me one hour of my life. If I wanted to buy a $240 car stereo, it would cost me 20 hours of my life.

(This way of thinking was a direct result of my method for planning my finances, which is described in Chapter 10.)

I later learned that I am not alone in thinking about money as time. So if I am crazy, at least I have company!

EXAMPLE

If I owe $2,000 and could only pay off $400 per month, it would take five months to pay off the entire debt.

As discussed earlier, if I make $10 per hour, the $2,000 bill is equivalent to 200 hours of my life (five forty-hour work weeks). However, we can also look at the $2,000 debt as being equal to the five months of my life required to pay off the debt.

Either way you look at it, money is time.

Money vs. Time

In a world where people depend on a salary for income, there is a direct correlation between time and money. You spend time at work to earn money. Therefore, when you spend money, you're spending the time it will take to earn that money.

So what should we value more, our money or our time?

Benjamin Franklin once said, "Do not waste time, for that is the stuff life is made of."

Life is time; time is life. We trade our time for money. The difference between time and money is: We can always earn more money, but once you've spent your time, you can never earn more.

Because it is irreplaceable, time—life—is more valuable.

Again, if I earn $12 per hour and want to buy something for $12, I am spending an hour of my life.

I qualify all potential purchases with two questions:

➤ How many hours do I have to work to pay for it?

➤ Is it worth that much of my life?

All of a sudden, that new car doesn't look so hot. That expensive leather jacket would cost a week of my life. Is it worth it? Often the answer is a resounding "No!"

When viewed through this filter, many of the things I have spent money on were not worth the time (life) required to pay for them.

So What Should We Do?

There's another problem with trading your time for money. You only have 24 hours a day. If you earn $10 an hour, your earnings are limited to $240 a day. Of course, you can't work 24 hours a day, so your earnings are limited even further.

Is there any way to change that?

There are ways to earn money without spending time (see Chapter 7). That is how many wealthy people become and stay wealthy. They have learned to leverage both their time and their money.

For now, it's important to remember that when you spend money, you are spending a part of your life that you can never get back.

CHAPTER 3

Possessions Are A Prison

—ↄɭɭↄ—

When was the best time of your life?

I would guess it's something like:

➤ The idyllic two weeks at summer camp when you were a child.

➤ The two-month backpacking trip across Europe.

➤ The trip to Mazatlan for spring break.

➤ The winter you spent at Sun Valley as a ski instructor.

➤ The family road trip across the United States when you were 12.

What's common among these experiences?

➤ You had the freedom to do whatever you wanted.

➤ You had few, if any, obligations.

➤ You were footloose and fancy-free.

➤ *You weren't burdened down with* STUFF.

Think about it. When you were at summer camp, you only had a duffle bag full of clothes, a toothbrush, and a couple of books. When you were backpacking around Europe, you only had a backpack full of necessities.

You weren't burdened down with *stuff*.

OK. I know. That's not the only reason you had fun. I'm sure the sun, the beach, the Parthenon, the skiing and the all-American landmarks added to the fun.

But not having to worry about a lot of stuff helped.

The latest travel trend espoused by experts, is to travel light. They suggest that whether you're going to Europe for three days or three months, you should only take one carry-on bag. That's it. One 22" x 14" x 9" bag. For three months of traveling.

Why? Because lugging around a bunch of suitcases, heavy with stuff, detracts from the fun of travel.

The same thing applies to our daily lives. We would all be happier with less stuff yet, if you look in the typical American home, our rooms, closets, garages, and attics are full of stuff. We bury ourselves in possessions.

The Hidden Cost of Possessions

Possessions cost money. You spend money when you buy stuff. Then you spend money to maintain, fix, store, clean, and move the stuff.

EXAMPLE

I once moved from one apartment to a smaller apartment. All my stuff wouldn't fit in the smaller apartment, so I "temporarily" put some of it in storage. The storage unit cost $70 per month, but I figured I would only need it for a couple of months. The couple of months stretched out to over a year. I actually forgot what was in the storage unit but, every month, I'd write a $70 check.

(Continues on next page)

(Continued from previous page)

I eventually got tired of writing the checks and went to the storage place to see what was in the unit. It turned out to be a bunch of junk. The total value of the stuff was maybe $500. I had spent over $840 to store $500 worth of stuff that I didn't even want!

Owning stuff not only costs money, it costs time and peace of mind. In addition to money, you spend time and energy storing stuff, cleaning it, maintaining it, fixing it, worrying about it, and moving it. When you're not actually spending time doing these things, you're probably thinking about them.

Remember, money is time and time is life.

We worry about or spend time:

➤ Changing the oil in the car(s).

➤ Cleaning the gutters.

➤ Fixing the lawn mower.

➤ Maintaining the bicycle.

➤ Buying a new propeller for the boat.

➤ Cleaning the mold off the deck.

➤ Fixing the pressure washer so we can clean the mold off the deck.

➤ Cleaning the BBQ grill.

➤ Replacing the light bulbs in the patio lights.

➤ Buying a washer for the leaking upstairs faucet.

➤ Getting our skis tuned.

➤ Sewing buttons back on our shirts.

The more stuff we have, the more worries and busywork we make for ourselves. The sad part is that we often don't really need or use the stuff.

How much time and life energy have you wasted on these activities?

How much would you have accomplished if you had spent this time working towards your goals? How much happier and more fulfilled would you be?

Possessions are a prison.

EXAMPLE

A big part of the American dream is owning your own home. The real estate industry has created a buzzword for your first home—it's your "starter home."

After a while, people get married, have children and "outgrow" their "starter homes" and upgrade to larger houses.

In the 1950s, the average home size was 983 square feet. The average family had 2.20 children.

In 2004, the average home size was 2,266 square feet and the average number of children per family was 1.89.

The size of families decreased by 14 percent, but the size of homes increased by 131 percent.

Why? Because we have a lot more stuff.

People accumulate so much stuff that they can no longer fit in the "starter home." They have to buy bigger houses with more closets and storage.

So what are the hidden costs of a larger home?

⋄ Higher maintenance bills

⋄ Higher heating and cooling bills

⋄ More carpet to vacuum

⋄ More lawn to mow

⋄ More garden to weed

⋄ More walls to paint

⋄ More bathrooms to clean

(Continues on next page)

(Continued from previous page)

✧ More things that can break

✧ And, of course, the larger mortgage

I don't know about you, but I can think of better ways to spend my weekends than cleaning an extra two bathrooms.

A larger home may provide more status and more room for your stuff, but it will also cost you more time and money.

When you decide to make any purchase, be sure that you are not only willing to pay the purchase price, but also the ongoing, hidden costs.

The Giant Marketing Machine

The ideas that "Possessions are a Prison" and "Debt is Slavery" are closely intertwined. Both debt and possessions can trap us and force us to do things we don't necessarily want to do.

We borrow money to buy things we don't need and don't use, which forces us to go to a job we hate so we can pay back the money we borrowed to buy things we don't need or use...

It's an endless cycle. Plus, there's a Giant Marketing Machine (GMM) out there working endlessly to convince us to spend our money and buy more stuff (I discuss the GMM in more detail in Chapter 4).

The GMM wants to reach into our pockets and take our money. It shows us how "celebrities" live, how much expensive stuff they own, and tries to convince us that we need to have that stuff too.

The GMM also convinces us that we have to buy and receive presents for:

➤ Christmas

➤ Father's Day

➤ Valentine's Day

➤ Birthdays

➤ Mother's Day

➤ Anniversaries

The GMM keeps coming up with new occasions to buy and receive presents. Often these presents are something we don't want or use. How many times have you bought something just because you needed to give someone a present? You will buy just about anything.

The interesting part is, we will often keep a present for years, even if we don't want it, need it, use it, or even know what the heck it is. We don't get rid of the item because it was a present from our Aunt Ethel.

The ironic part is, Aunt Ethel, needing to buy a birthday present, may not have put a lot of thought into her gift. She may have bought the first thing she saw at the store.

When you want to get rid of the stuff, you have a garage sale and spend a weekend of your life moving, cleaning, and tagging stuff so people can come in and offer pennies on the dollar for your precious possessions. Whatever you don't sell, you have to haul to Goodwill. What a way to spend your free time!

I'm not saying that garage sales are bad. But if we control the stuff that enters our lives, we can minimize the time and energy spent getting rid of it, and do something more fun, fulfilling, and productive.

EXAMPLE

My girlfriend and I decided to take up scuba diving. We took the course and became certified.

Thinking that diving was something I would do often, I bought all the gear: wetsuit, tank, regulator, fins, dive computer—the works.

I spent a couple of thousand dollars and how often did I use the gear?

Three times.

I also bought myself ongoing bills.

(Continues on next page)

(Continued from previous page)

Scuba tanks have to be inspected and re-certified every year. Regulators need to be serviced.

I kept the gear in my cluttered garage and every time I had to get something out of the back of the garage, I bruised my shins on the tank.

I finally bit the bullet and sold the gear. I haven't missed it since.

Put Stuff Back Into Circulation

I have difficulty getting rid of stuff. A lot of my stuff is in very good condition, and even if I haven't used it for years, I think "I should keep that" because:

➤ It's in great shape.

➤ It would cost a lot of money to replace.

➤ I may need it someday.

I recently came up with a philosophical approach to deal with this problem. It is better to put an item "back into circulation" by selling or giving it to someone who will use it.

EXAMPLE
A while ago, I decided to learn how to play the guitar. I never got really good at playing the guitar, but I did manage to get "guitar fever," which is the desire to own more than one guitar. I eventually had four guitars, which filled up my entire downstairs closet.

I soon lost interest in the guitar, but for some reason, I wanted to keep all four of my guitars even though I rarely played them. It was unlikely that I'd ever take the time to practice and learn to play them well.

(Continues on next page)

(Continued from previous page)

I eventually put three of the guitars up for sale. In every case, the person who bought the guitar was an avid musician who would get a lot of use out of it.

I cleared out my closet by putting my guitars "back into circulation." Somewhere, someone is enjoying the beautiful music they are playing, music that would never have existed if my guitars had remained silent in the dusty confines of my downstairs closet.

EXAMPLE

One Halloween, I decided to have the best-decorated house in the neighborhood. As part of my plan, I bought a fog machine.

Owning a fog machine had hidden costs. What I didn't realize was:

- ✧ Fog juice is expensive.
- ✧ The fog machine needs to be cleaned regularly.
- ✧ Cleaning solution is expensive.
- ✧ I wanted the fog to hug the ground as an eerie mist. In order to do that, I needed to build a "fog chiller." I had to buy a large cooler, some chicken wire, some PVC piping, a hole saw, and some clamps.

Having an eerie mist covering the front lawn for Halloween was fun, but the fog machine and chiller took up too much space in the garage, especially since I only used them once a year.

I decided to put my fog machine "back into circulation." I eventually sold it to an aspiring DJ who will use it weekly.

I cleared out space in my garage and the fog machine is contributing to people's fun at some party somewhere, instead of being on a shelf in my garage.

Accomplish and Achieve, Don't Accumulate

Our society focuses on accumulating possessions. Somehow, owning certain stuff is supposed to give us self-worth. We are subjected to lies like "you are what you drive" or "if you don't wear this brand of clothes, you're nobody".

We spend our lives working to make money to buy stuff, which gives us a momentary feeling of satisfaction and then the feeling's gone.

We buy a new BMW, but next year, BMW comes out with a new model and we're no longer satisfied with the old one. So we sell the old BMW and buy a new one. The following year, BMW comes out with a new model and...

It's an endless cycle of meaningless consumption.

Don't define your self-worth by what you own. Instead, concentrate on accumulating accomplishments and experiences, not stuff. Stuff can be stolen, broken, or destroyed.

Nobody can take away what we accomplish.

EXAMPLE

John bases his self-worth on what he owns. He prides himself on always having the latest electronic gadget. He despises obsolescence.

John is proud of his new 3.2 megapixel digital camera. It's small, about the size of a deck of cards, and has 128MB of memory. He shows it off to all his neighbors and friends.

One day, John's neighbor drops by to show off his new camera. It's a 5.0 megapixel camera that's half the size of John's and has 1.0 gigabytes of memory.

John can't stand that his neighbor has a better camera than he does, so he rushes to the store and buys a 6.0 megapixel camera with 2.0 gigabytes of memory. It costs him $500, but that's OK because John uses his Visa.

(Continues on next page)

(Continued from previous page)

John will never have the latest electronic gadget. Technology advances so quickly that products are obsolete almost as soon as they hit the shelves.

Basing your self-esteem on what you own is bad enough, but financing your habit with debt is even worse.

We are not what we own; we are what we do. Our achievements define us—what we do tells people who we are—and, unlike possessions, our accomplishments can give us real satisfaction and real self-worth.

As we get older, we will remember what we've done in our lives, not what we've owned, because life is about doing, not having.

Focus on accumulating experiences, accomplishments, and achievements, not stuff.

Rules to Control the Stuff in Your Life

1. Don't be "big hat, no cattle."

If you ever visit Texas, you might hear someone say, "He's big hat and no cattle."

Someone is "big hat and no cattle" when they look successful and prosperous (by wearing a big hat), but aren't (they don't own any cattle).

Just because someone drives a BMW doesn't mean they're rich and successful. Anybody can lease a BMW for only a few hundred dollars a month. There are a lot of people who drive Mercedes Benzes but live in shacks. They wear Rolexes, but can barely pay their phone bill.

There's a certain joy to being low-key; to not drive a Mercedes, but know you can write a check and buy one. That's economic and financial freedom.

You should strive to be "no hat, but *lots* of cattle."

2. If you don't need it—don't buy it.

We all buy stuff we don't need. We go to the store and see a gadget we must have. We think, "I may as well buy it now because I'm sure to need it sometime in the future *and* it's 50 percent off!"

But your closets and garage are full of stuff you didn't need but bought anyhow. And guess what? You never used it.

3. If you don't use it—get rid of it.

How much stuff is in your closets and garage right now that you haven't used in over a year?

Get rid of the stuff you don't need or use. You'll feel a lot better. Pack it up and take it to Goodwill. Or if you want, have a garage sale. Put the stuff "back into circulation."

Getting rid of stuff is very liberating.

4. Don't love something that can't love you back.

I have friends who define their self-worth on what kind of car they drive. They just love their car.

But is that love returned?

When you love a thing, the love will never be returned. A car will never comfort you when you're sick. It will never help you when you're in trouble. If you're going to love something, make sure it can love you back.

5. Give experiences instead of gifts.

Do you want to give a gift that someone will appreciate and possibly remember for the rest of their lives?

Then give experiences instead of gifts.

Instead of buying your dad a tie with a golf ball painted on it, why not treat him to a round of golf at a local course or buy him a private lesson?

Instead of owning a tie that he will never wear, you may create a memory he will cherish for a lifetime.

Which do you think he'd rather have?

6. Learn how to have "no money required" fun.

You don't have to spend money to have fun. Learn to have "no money required" fun.

It's hard to have "no money required" fun nowadays. Everything costs money. You have to drive somewhere, you have to buy some food. But you don't have to spend $50 a ticket to go to a baseball game, or $10 each to see a movie.

> ➤ Go for a walk in the park.

> ➤ Take a drive in the country.

> ➤ Go hiking.

> ➤ Check out a guidebook from your local library and play tourist in your own town.

> ➤ Instead of skiing, go sledding.

> ➤ Go fishing.

> ➤ Play some pick-up basketball with friends.

Get creative with your fun. You don't have to accept the pre-packaged fun that the GMM has created for you.

8. Life is meant to be lived, not preserved.

I like to take photos, especially if they capture a special moment in time. It is nice to look at old photos and reminisce. However, there's a danger that we can become so concerned about *preserving* a moment in time, that we don't fully *live* the moment in time.

I have witnessed people who are so busy videotaping or photographing their vacation that they miss out on the full vacation experience. It's as if they spend their entire vacation recording everything, so that they can enjoy it after they get home.

The same thing happens at weddings, baptisms, graduations, and birthday parties. People are so busy preserving the moment that they don't experience the richness of the event.

We fill our closets and the spaces under the beds with boxes and crates full of videotapes and photographs that we never look at, but "someday" intend to put in albums or on DVDs.

Life is meant to be lived. Don't waste your life trying to capture moments in time, so you can preserve them like flies in amber.

9. *Evaluate purchases based on how much value you will extract.*

As we've discussed earlier, you can evaluate purchases by calculating how much of your time (life) it would cost.

Another way to evaluate a purchase is: How much value will you get out of it?

For example, I used to have a weakness for buying CDs on impulse. I'd see a CD in a store, purchase it, listen to it once or twice, stick it on a shelf, and never listen to it again. My shelves became filled with CDs until I eventually decided to get rid of some.

Have you ever tried to sell a used CD? A new CD costs around $12. A store will offer you maybe $2 for the CD. Your CD loses 83 percent of its value as soon as the wrapper is removed.

It's OK to pay $12 for a CD if you will listen to it often enough to get $12 of value out of it. But if you will never listen to the CD, you just wasted $10 ($12 minus $2). The same phenomenon applies to clothes, DVDs, furniture, books, and knickknacks.

✻ So, before you buy something, make sure you'll get the purchase price's worth of use out of it, otherwise you're just wasting your money.

10. Be a creator, not a consumer.

Anyone can buy a $2,000 vintage Fender Stratocaster guitar, but can they play it?

Which is better, owning the most expensive tennis racket money can buy or winning the local tournament?

Instead of buying a $200 pair of basketball shoes, why not dedicate another 30 minutes a day to practicing ball-handling?

Instead of buying a new iPod, why not keep the old one and consider writing your own songs or taking some music or voice lessons?

I am not saying that everyone should stop buying stuff. There's nothing wrong with owning a $2,000 electric guitar. And not everybody will win the local tennis tournament.

But it's much more satisfying to be a creator than a consumer. We should focus on improving our skills and abilities, not increasing our stack of possessions.

Conclusion

Possessions are a prison—a prison we build for ourselves and can easily escape.

It's time for your jailbreak!

—ɯ—

CHAPTER 4

Be Aware of the Ongoing Campaign to Separate You from Your Money

—⟋⟍—

There is an ongoing campaign to separate you from your money. You may not be aware of it, but it exists and is constantly trying to influence the way you think—to brainwash you into handing over your money.

What am I? Some kind of conspiracy nut?

No, I'm not talking about some dark government conspiracy. I'm talking about the advertising industry, or as I like to call it: the Giant Marketing Machine (GMM).

> **Brainwashing:**
>
> *1) Intensive indoctrination aimed at changing a person's basic convictions and attitudes and replacing them with a fixed and unquestioned set of beliefs.*
>
> *2) Indoctrination or persuasion by advertising or salesmanship.*

Ad agencies and marketing companies are paid incredible amounts of money to market products. Their sole purpose is to manipulate us into spending our money on their clients' products.

How do they do this?

➤ They try to convince us that we can't live without their product.

➤ They try to convince us that buying their product will improve our lives. They may link the product with a desirable lifestyle or with beautiful people. They'll say, "If you buy my product, you can be beautiful too!" or "If you buy my product, look at all the fun you'll have!"

➤ They constantly expose us to advertising. Count how many advertisements you encounter in a typical day:

Advertising exists:

✦ On the radio.

✦ On television.

✦ On the sides of public buses.

✦ In movies and TV shows. (Advertisers pay to have their products prominently displayed in movies and TV shows. This is called "product placement." The next time you see a movie character drinking Coke instead of Pepsi, realize that Coke probably paid a lot of money for that privilege.)

✦ On billboards.

✦ In magazines and newspapers.

✦ On clothing. (I can't believe how much money people pay to become billboards for some clothing designer.)

✦ Before movies.

✦ In songs.

We have become so desensitized to advertising that we are unaware of its insidious effect on our lives. We have become sheep who buy what we are told to buy.

Isn't that a little extreme? Are we really sheep?

So what kind of clothes are "in"? What kind of car should you drive if you want to look successful?

How do you know what's "cool" and what's not?

Advertisers and marketers tell you.

Advertisers are hired to convince us to spend our hard-earned money on their clients' products. They want to put their hands in our wallets and take our money.

Remember, money is time. It's your time. Time is life. It's ✳ your life.

When you spend money, you're making yourself poorer and somebody else richer.

Have you ever seen one of those celebrity "lifestyle" shows on TV? Did you wonder how celebrities can afford their mansions, Rolls Royces, yachts, diamond jewelry, and swimming pools?

They use *your* money.

When you buy a CD, a DVD, or designer clothes, that money finds its way to the celebrity. The celebrity then spends that money to buy Bentleys and Jaguars. In the meantime, you're driving your 10-year-old Ford Escort.

Their Ferraris, private jets, and mansions were paid for with *your hard-earned cash*. Think about how much you overpaid for their products if they can live that kind of lifestyle.

Then go back to your job so you can earn money to pay your bills.

Status/Fashion

People often buy things because they are concerned with "status" or "being in fashion."

Someone once told me that "status" is "buying things you don't need to impress people you don't know."

That's an astute statement.

American society is focused on status. We want to impress not only our friends, but everyone else, including a lot of people we don't know.

The GMM has brainwashed us into thinking that owning certain stuff will give us status. For example, we are told that we have status, that we're "cool" if we:

➤ Drive a Lexus, BMW, or Mercedes.

➤ Golf.

➤ Wear "Sean Jean" clothes.

➤ Go trekking in Nepal.

➤ Exercise by doing Pilates.

➤ Live in a 3,500+ square foot home.

➤ Eat at the "right" restaurants.

➤ Shop at the "right" stores.

➤ Own a plasma TV.

➤ Listen to "50 Cent."

➤ Have a tattoo.

(Note that by the time you read this book, "Sean Jean" clothes may be out-of-fashion, "50 Cent" may no longer have a best-selling CD, Nepal may no longer be the "hot" vacation spot, and Pilates may have gone the way of "Jazzercise". That's how transient "fashion" is.)

How many people wear "leg-warmers" today? Or "Members Only" jackets? When was the last time you saw someone wearing "Gloria Vanderbilt" jeans? Or sporting a haircut like those guys in "Flock of Seagulls?" All of these things were fashionable once. Today, they're fodder for jokes.

The GMM defines what is fashionable and what is not. Its ubiquitous advertising and marketing affects how we think and what we buy—*if we allow it.*

The music and clothing industries must continually offer new products and convince us to buy them. Ironically, they do this by telling us that what they convinced us to buy yesterday is no longer "in." We are constantly bombarded with lists telling us what's "in" and what's "out."

The GMM wants you to spend your hard-earned money on its overpriced junk. Then it wants you to throw away yesterday's overpriced junk so you can spend your hard-earned money on today's overpriced junk.

Why fall into their trap? Don't be a chump.

Conclusion

Don't let advertising brainwash you. Be aware that the GMM is constantly trying to influence how you spend your money.

Control your mind and your thoughts in order to control your money and your life.

—∿—

CHAPTER 5

Money Buys Freedom

—w—

"Money does not buy happiness."

Everyone's heard that cliché a million times. But is it true?

Have you ever heard someone say something like:

- ➤ "If I had a bigger house, I'd be happy."

- ➤ "Once I buy a Mercedes, I'll be happy."

- ➤ "After I retire and buy a house on the beach, I'll be happy."

- ➤ "If I owned a private jet, I'd be happy."

- ➤ "Once I buy a boat, I'll be happy."

- ➤ "If I had an RV, I'd travel around the country and I'd be happy."

Have you personally had similar thoughts?

Some people believe that if they had a lot of money, they could buy a lot of stuff and then they'd be happy.

But we've learned that possessions are a prison and cannot provide happiness. They may provide momentary satisfaction, but they do not provide happiness.

So, in that context, the old saying is true.

However, can money buy something other than stuff?

Money can buy freedom, options, and opportunity. And freedom, options, and opportunity can lead to happiness.

Money can also buy peace of mind. How you handle your money can have a positive effect on your life, peace of mind, and well-being.

EXAMPLE

Let's look at the financial profiles of two people:

Jill: Makes $35,000 a year.

Has $250 in her savings account.

Owes $10,000 on her credit cards.

Joan: Makes $35,000 a year.

Has $10,000 in her savings account.

Owes $250 on her credit cards.

Who do you think sleeps better at night? Who has more peace of mind?

If you:

➤ Control your expenses (see Chapter 8),

➤ Maximize your savings,

➤ Minimize your possessions,

➤ Create a passive income (see Chapter 7),

you can:

➤ Take six months off to travel the world.

➤ Take six weeks off without pay to write a book (like I'm doing right now).

➤ Go back to school full-time for one, two, or four years to study something you really enjoy.

➤ Take time off to volunteer for a political campaign.

➤ Not take the first job that comes along because you're desperate for money.

Many of us don't like our jobs. Our jobs are often unfulfilling, but we continue to go back because we need the money. If we had enough money, we would walk away from our jobs and do something we really wanted to do. We would pursue our dreams of traveling the world, or being a writer, a musician, a philanthropist, a gourmet cook, or a scratch golfer. We would go back to school to get our Masters, MBA, law degree, or PhD, or become an MD or DDS.

We would do these things if we had enough money. Because money buys freedom, options, and opportunity.

Retirement

A common misconception about retirement is that it has something to do with age. People believe you have to be 55, 62 or 65 years old to retire.

Retirement has nothing to do with age. It has *everything* to do with money.

A social phenomenon that emerged in the 1990s is the number of people in their 20s and 30s who quit their jobs after receiving windfalls from company stock options. They made so much money that they "retired," quitting their jobs to pursue lives of leisure, travel, philanthropy, or chasing dreams.

In the past, people worked at a job—usually with the same company—for 30, 40, or 50 years before they were able to collect their company pension and retire. People didn't get stock options back then, so they didn't have the opportunity to become overnight millionaires and walk away from their jobs.

The reason we think that 55, 62, or 65 is a magic age is, in the past, you couldn't collect your company pension and Social Security until you reached those ages. With most companies doing away with or limiting company pension plans, these ages no longer have the same significance.

If you won a multi-million-dollar lottery today, would you go back to work tomorrow? The majority of people would be happy to tell their bosses to take a hike.

That's because retirement is about money, not age.

Conclusion

Money may not buy happiness, but it does buy freedom, options, and opportunity—and freedom, options, and opportunity may lead to happiness.

So the next time you pull out your wallet or credit card to make a purchase, think about the freedom you're spending, because money is not only time, it is also your freedom.

—ɯ—

CHAPTER 6

Don't Sell Your Soul for A Salary

—◊◊◊—

A few years ago, a friend told me how stressed he was about work. I suggested he go on vacation when he finished his project. He had six weeks saved up, so why not take a two- or three-week vacation to unwind?

His reply? "I never enjoy vacations because I know it's only temporary. If I take a two-week vacation, I'm aware, as each day passes, I'm closer and closer to going back to work."

Wow. That's pretty extreme. Or is he being honest?

I think we have all experienced the dread of returning to work after time off, whether for a vacation, a holiday, or a weekend. The dread can either make you savor your free time more, or destroy the enjoyment of that free time.

Do you enjoy Sunday nights? Sunday nights fill many people with dread because they know they have to go back to work Monday morning.

So why do we end up at jobs we don't like?

Because we sold our souls for a salary.

How Many People Like Their Jobs?

I use the phrase "the job you hate" a few times in this book. But maybe you don't hate your job. Maybe you like your job.

In fact, a recent poll of U.S. workers determined that about 60 percent of employees are satisfied with their jobs to some extent. That sounds a little high to me (although it does mean that 40 percent are *dissatisfied* with their jobs).

Why am I skeptical?

Take an informal poll among your friends. First ask them if they like their jobs. Then ask them, "If you won a $100 million lottery tonight, would you quit your job?"

I'd bet an overwhelming majority of them will answer "yes, they'd quit their jobs if they won the lottery", even if they answered the previous question with "yes, they like their jobs" (and it'll probably be a lot more than 40 percent).

I think a lot of people say they like their jobs when, in reality, they have merely resigned themselves to the fact that they have to work to pay the bills.

So, maybe most people don't "hate" their jobs. But most people would choose to do something different if they were financially free and independent of money worries.

How We Choose Our Careers

Here are some ways people choose their careers:

1) Someone once told them, "Hey, you should be a _____." Common examples would be "Hey, you like to argue, you should be a lawyer," or "Hey, you're good at math, you should be an engineer."

2) They studied for a career without really knowing what the job entailed.

3) Their parents always wanted them to be a _____.

4) They fell into it.

5) They took a "temporary" job, got comfortable, and never left.

6) They needed the money, took the first job that came down the pike, and stayed for 40 years.

Most people take jobs because they need or want the money. We often take the job that pays the most because, well, we all want to make more money.

The problem is, if, when considering a job, our top priority is the size of the salary, we may end up with a job or career we don't like. Then, if our lifestyle and spending habits expand to consume our entire salary, it's difficult to change careers to something we may enjoy more, but which pays less.

Also, there is a limit to how far we can go if we either don't enjoy or aren't interested in our jobs. We just won't put in the time and effort required to advance. If you are interested in your job, you'll work harder, improve your skills, and there's no limit to how far you can go.

In general, Americans spend eight hours a day, five days a week, at work. If we account for commuting time and lunch breaks, we spend 10 hours a day on our jobs.

If 50 hours a week is spent at our jobs and 49 hours a week (7x7) is spent sleeping, that means 42 percent of our waking time each week is spent at our jobs (a week has 168 hours).

Why would we want to spend 42 percent of our lives doing something we don't enjoy?

We are wasting our time and our lives. What could you accomplish if you took 10 hours a day and devoted it to something for which you had a passion? Wouldn't your life and the world be a better place? Why not devote our time and lives to something we are passionate about?

Because we sell our souls for a salary.

EXAMPLE

In high school, someone told me, "you're good at math, you should be an engineer."

So I decided to be a civil engineer. I liked the idea of designing roads, bridges, and skyscrapers.

Then one of my teachers talked me out of it. "There's no future in civil engineering," he said. "How many new bridges, roads, and buildings do we need?"

Being a trusting high school student, I decided not to become a civil engineer.

Instead, I decided to become a computer programmer. I had studied computer programming in school. I enjoyed it. I was good at it.

Then, a college guidance counselor told me "don't major in computer science, there are no jobs. That fad is over."

OK. So I won't be a computer science major.

I told him that I thought about becoming an English teacher. The same counselor who talked me out of computer programming told me that English teachers weren't in demand and made no money.

The counselor then told me that with my good grades and excellence in math, I should get a Mechanical Engineering degree. Mechanical Engineers were in demand and they commanded a high starting salary.

So I majored in Mechanical Engineering. I did well in my classes, but didn't really enjoy them. I had no passion for engineering.

I earned a Bachelor of Science in Mechanical Engineering and ended up working in the aerospace industry. It's been fun and I've had some interesting experiences, but I still wonder what I could have accomplished if I had pursued a career for which I had greater passion (like writing!)

(Continues on next page)

(Continued from previous page)

That's how I planned my career and I don't think I'm an exception.

(Do you remember the two criteria I had for choosing a teacher? My experience getting bad advice from people like my high school teacher and college guidance counselor helped me create those criteria.)

So How Should We Choose Our Jobs?

If we're going to spend 42 percent of our waking time at our jobs, maybe we should:

➤ Do something we enjoy and are interested in, not just what pays.

➤ Find a job that lines up with our beliefs, values, and life goals.

We need to do more research when choosing a career, like finding out exactly what a job entails. For example, how many of you spoke with someone who did the job you were considering? Did you talk to an engineer to see what she does on a daily basis? Or a lawyer? A doctor? A teacher?

EXAMPLE

My nephew once asked me what I did for a living.

"I'm an aerospace design engineer," I replied.

"You design airplanes?"

I nodded.

He seemed impressed. "What exactly do you do?"

"I design airframe structure for commercial jets."

"But what do you do?" *(Continues on next page)*

(Continued from previous page)

"Right now, I'm designing skins for a new commercial jet derivative."

"No," he said. "What do you do every day? Describe exactly what you do when you walk into the office every morning."

"Well, I log into my computer, check my calendar for meetings and check my e-mail. Then I check my voice mail. If I have a meeting, I go to it. If not, I log into our CAD program and..."

I knew I was losing him. Somehow the daily reality of my job didn't sound as impressive as he had imagined. I'm sure he thought I was out on the airfield talking to test pilots or something.

Before I finished my description, he had obviously lost interest.

This kid knew what to ask. He wanted to know exactly what an aerospace design engineer does on a daily basis.

I sure wish I had asked the same questions before choosing my career.

Other Considerations

What about taking a job because of what you'll learn from it? Maybe that should be the primary consideration, not the size of the salary. Jobs can be stepping stones to your ultimate goals. Evaluate them accordingly.

The earnings will come as you learn and grow. To maximize this potential, choose a career that you enjoy.

We should also realize that a job or career is not static. We often feel "trapped" because we believe we have too much time invested in our current job; "I've been here for 20 years, how can I change?"

Don't be afraid to take one step backward to take two steps forward. You may have to take a salary cut when changing to a more fulfilling career. The impact of a pay cut is minimized if you're in stable financial condition. Chapter 10 will show you concrete ways to gain control of your money.

Conclusion

Don't make money the primary objective when choosing a career. If you work at something for which you have a passion, you can create a niche for yourself, where you are an expert in your field and where your earnings potential can be limitless. Then you will be one of the few truly fulfilled individuals who work doing what they love to do.

If you can improve your relationship with money, gain control over your finances, and free yourself from the insidious influence of the Giant Marketing Machine, you can be free to choose your career according to your interests, not your monthly bills.

Don't sell your soul for a salary.

—⋙—

CHAPTER 7

Own

—w—

How do people gain financial independence? How do they buy their freedom? How do people become wealthy in the United States and how do they stay wealthy?

They *own*.

Say what? Wealthy people "own"? But didn't we decide that "Possessions are a Prison?"

Well, some possessions are a prison. Others aren't.

I'm sure you're thinking, "That sure sounds like a cop-out!"

Don't worry. I'll explain what I mean.

So what do wealthy people own?

If you were a multi-millionaire, how would you spend your money? What would you buy from the following list?

Pick four.

1) Diamond jewelry

2) A Ferrari

3) A yacht

4) Commercial real estate

5) A Rolex

6) A Bentley

7) A private jet

8) A world-class Thoroughbred
9) A new wardrobe of the latest designer clothes
10) An original Picasso
11) A waterfront mansion
12) A plastic injection-molding company
13) A nightclub
14) A trucking company
15) A limousine
16) A chalet at Aspen
17) A gold-plated Hummer with spinners
18) The publishing rights to the Beatles' song catalog.

You've probably sensed a trap—and you're right.

Income-Producing Assets vs. Income-Consuming Assets

The list includes two kinds of assets: income-producing and income-consuming. If you want financial freedom, you should accumulate the former and avoid the latter.

So there it is. The difference between possessions that become a prison and possessions that set you free is this:

➤ Income-consuming assets trap you.

➤ Income-producing assets set you free.

So how does the list break down?

➤ Income-producing: 4, 12, 13, 14, 18

➤ Income-consuming: 1, 2, 3, 5, 6, 7, 8, 9, 10, 11, 15, 16, 17

But, why would the Picasso be income-consuming?

It costs a lot of money to maintain a valuable, old painting. It needs to be stored in a controlled environment. It also needs to have a robust security system to prevent it from being stolen or damaged. In addition, you will probably have to carry expensive insurance to protect the painting from damage or theft.

But wouldn't the Picasso increase in value over time? Maybe, but it does not produce income. It only produces a profit when it is sold. In the meantime, it is consuming income. The same thing applies to non-rental real estate such as a primary home or a vacation home (e.g. a waterfront mansion or chalet in Aspen). Personal real estate may appreciate over time, but it does not produce income. It consumes income because you have to spend money on maintenance, utilities, repairs, taxes, and insurance. The only way you can extract money from real estate is by taking out a home-equity loan (debt!) or by selling the property.

Wealthy people own. They own businesses, stocks, bonds, and real estate. These assets produce income on which they can live. Wealthy people can live without trading their time for money. Most wealthy people, especially if they're self-made, are aware of the difference between income-producing assets and income-consuming assets.

Concentrate on accumulating income-producing assets and eventually you too can join the ranks of the financially free. Own enough income-producing assets to pay for your income-consuming ones. Concentrate on gaining control of your money and your life.

EXAMPLE

Isn't rental property always an "income-producing asset"?

No.

Rental property does produce an income, but if the income isn't large enough to cover expenses, it is an "income-consuming asset."

If you decide to accumulate rental property, make sure that the income, at minimum, covers total expenses (don't forget about hidden costs). Ideally, you'll want the rental income to exceed expenses by a comfortable margin.

EXAMPLE

I recently thought about buying a sailboat. I found one that seemed like a screaming bargain. It was a very nice 26-foot sailboat, it was in great shape, and the seller was asking only $4,000 for it.

Yet, he was having problems selling the boat.

Why?

The boat was not easily towable on a trailer because it was very heavy and had a "fixed keel." The owner had it moored in a local marina for $270 a month.

Whoever bought the boat couldn't easily store it anyplace but in a marina. They would probably want to continue the existing moorage contract because it was the best deal around for in-the-water moorage.

Whoever bought the boat would not only buy the boat, but also a $270 ongoing monthly bill. That didn't include the cost to license, maintain, and insure the boat.

There were a lot of hidden expenses for whoever bought the boat, but many people wouldn't look at the big picture. All they would see is the cheap selling price for the boat.

This sailboat is the perfect example of an income-consuming asset. Sure, the boat would be fun, but whoever buys it better be sure that the additional monthly expenses are worth it.

Financial Windfalls

How many people, when they receive a financial windfall, go out and buy a new car? Or take an expensive vacation? Or buy a plasma television? A boat? A motorcycle?

Instead of preparing for a future of financial freedom, people will spend a one-time windfall on something that will immediately lose most of its value. That is why lottery winners often end up broke. They buy income-consuming assets that eventually consume all of their winnings.

If you receive a one-time windfall, use some of it to treat yourself. But it's wise to also bolster your future financial independence.

How To Earn Money Without Spending Time

To gain freedom from financial concerns, you need to create "passive income", which is earning money without having to trade your time for money.

So how can you earn money without spending time? Own an income-producing asset.

You can earn money, without spending time, from:

➤ Interest on a savings or money market account.

➤ Stock dividends.

➤ Certificates of Deposit (CDs)

➤ Full or partial ownership of a business.

➤ Rental property.

➤ Royalties from a book, song, or patent.

You can accumulate enough income-producing assets to replace your work income. Then you can earn money without spending time.

That is the kind of freedom money can buy.

Stocks

So what about stocks? Aren't they a good asset to own?

They can be. The right stocks can appreciate significantly and make you wealthy, but most stocks do not pay dividends and thus do not qualify as income-producing assets.

Owning stocks is an essential part of any investment portfolio, but investing in stocks is beyond the scope of this book. There are many fine books (and many more poor ones) on how to invest in stocks and I will defer to them.

Possibly the Worst Way You Can Spend Your Money

I have an investment proposal for you. Here's my sales pitch:

➤ You will probably need to take out a five- or six-year loan to participate.

➤ The investment will *immediately* lose 5 to 10 percent of its value.

➤ It will lose 15–30 percent of its value in the first year.

➤ It will cost 5 to 10 percent in annual expense fees.

➤ It will lose 60–90 percent in value in five or six years.

Would you participate in this investment?

Of course not.

Yet, people spend their money on this investment all the time.

What is it?

It's buying a car.

Buying a car is possibly the worst way you can spend your money. Cars are probably the most common income-consuming assets.

So why do we continue to throw our money away on cars?

Most of us need cars to get around. Although any car can get us from point A to point B, we're not willing to buy just *any* car.

The Giant Marketing Machine (GMM, see Chapter 4) has convinced us, through endless advertising, that the car we drive defines who we are.

No longer is a car just a form of transportation, it is also an accessory. No one in their right mind would drive up to an elegant, expensive restaurant in a beat-up Hyundai. You'd be laughed out of the restaurant. You have to own at least a BMW or Mercedes.

Or so they've brainwashed us to think.

The Best Way to Buy a Car

The problem with cars is that most of us need one for transportation. So how should we handle "the worst possible way to spend our money?"

There are many books and articles about how to buy a car. One common suggestion is to buy a car that is two or three years old, since cars lose most of their value during that time.

I disagree. How a car is maintained in its first two or three years can determine its reliability for the rest of its life.

If you can afford it, I believe it's better to buy a new car and keep it for a minimum of eight to ten years.

As long as you take care of it, a new car will provide much more reliable transportation than a used car—without the unexpected repairs that can throw a wrench in your financial plans.

Services like "Consumer Reports New Car Price Reports" can tell you exactly what a dealer paid for a new car. You can negotiate from there and get a very good deal. I have bought *new* cars for less than what one- or two-year old models were selling for.

When you buy a new car, you know its history—there isn't any. It's brand new. You know it hasn't been wrecked and it hasn't been abused. You can control the quality of its maintenance.

If you do buy a new car, you must diligently perform the required maintenance, otherwise, the car will cause you problems in the future.

In my opinion, the best way to buy a car is to:

1) Buy it new.

2) Negotiate a good deal using the guidelines in "Consumer Reports New Car Price Reports".

3) Maintain the car properly.

4) Keep it for a minimum of eight to ten years or—as a friend once told me—"until the wheels fall off."

Conclusion

Money can buy freedom. We don't have to trade our time for money. We can earn money without spending time (life).

We can do this by realizing there are two kinds of assets: income-producing and income-consuming.

Income-consuming assets can imprison us.

Income-producing assets can set us free.

CHAPTER 8

Spend Less Than You Earn By Controlling Your Expenses

—⁓—

Sounds obvious, doesn't it? But it can be harder than it sounds. In order to "spend less than you earn," you have to value your peace of mind and financial security more than the things you can buy.

We've already learned that debt is slavery and that possessions can be a prison. We know that when we spend money, we're also spending our time and life. We're aware of the Giant Marketing Machine that constantly tries to brainwash us into wanting more and more stuff, which leads to more and more bills.

By incorporating these lessons into our financial lives, we can gain control of our money. These lessons will give us the power to say "No!" to unnecessary spending and expenses.

The Two Different Kinds of Expenses

First, we have to be aware of the two kinds of expenses: one-time expenses and ongoing expenses.

One-time expenses are just that, one-time. You pay it, and it's gone. An example of a one-time expense is if your car transmission breaks. You get it fixed, pay the bill, and then it's done.

An ongoing expense would be something like a subscription for cable TV, internet service, newspapers and magazines. Your rent, as well as monthly electricity, phone, gas and water/sewer/ garbage bills are also ongoing expenses.

An example of creating an ongoing expense is getting a dog. When you own a dog, you have to buy food, pay vet bills, and buy carpet shampoo. By getting a dog, you create a lot of ongoing expenses.

Ongoing expenses are becoming more and more common. Companies are creating "subscription" services that require monthly payments, where the service either used to be free or only required a one-time payment.

An example of a new "subscription" service is satellite radio. All radio used to be free. Now, you have to pay a monthly fee for satellite radio. Of course, satellite radio does provide a larger variety of stations and commercial-free stations, but it is a subscription-based alternative to what used to be free.

Think about all the bills that didn't exist 20 years ago:

1) Cellular phone service
2) Internet access
3) Satellite radio
4) Tivo
5) Satellite TV
6) Cable TV
7) Netflix

Today, these are "can't live without them" bills. Not only that, they are ongoing bills. We pay them each month, only to have to pay them again next month.

We go to work every day—to jobs we hate—to pay these bills.

Raises

Raises. We all want them; we all want to make more money. But what happens when people get a raise?

Often, they will:

➤ Buy a more expensive car.

➤ Buy a bigger house.

➤ Buy a boat.

➤ Buy a vacation home.

➤ Buy a bigger TV.

➤ Join expensive health or country clubs.

They adopt a more expensive lifestyle, increase their expenses and spend the raise. They're making more money, but they're still not getting ahead. They sell their souls for a salary, become debt and wage slaves, then increase their bondage by adding more bills and expenses.

There is a better way to handle your raise.

Controlling Your Expenses Has a Wonderful Effect on Your Savings

In order to achieve financial security and peace, *don't let your expenses increase with your income.* There's a powerful phenomenon that can happen when you make more money. If you control your expenses, the amount you save will increase by greater multiples than the percentage of your raise.

EXAMPLE

1) You make $50,000 per year.

2) Your expenses are $45,000 per year.

3) You save $5,000 per year ($50,000 – $45,000).

(Continues on next page)

(Continued from previous page)

4) You get a 10 percent raise.

5) How much more can you save?

Salary	Expenses	Savings	% Increase in Salary	% Increase in Savings
$50,000	$45,000	$5,000	0%	0%
$55,000	$45,000	$10,000	10%	100%
$60,000	$45,000	$15,000	20%	200%
$65,000	$45,000	$20,000	30%	300%

(Note: For simplicity's sake, I'm ignoring the effect of taxes on your salary.)

The 10 percent raise equals $5,000 per year. If your expenses stay the same, you should be able to save $10,000 per year.

Your salary increased by only 10 percent, but your savings didn't increase by 10 percent, they doubled!

This will only happen if *control your expenses.*

Minimizing Your Monthly Bills

How can we minimize monthly bills?

1) Eliminate debt.

 Once we eliminate debt, we minimize the monthly payments needed to service that debt.

2) Evaluate each monthly bill to see if you are getting value for your money.

Chapter 10 will show you exactly how to plan your finances and visually keep track of monthly bills.

Here are some other ideas for lowering your expenses:

➤ Instead of paying a monthly bill for voice mail, buy an inexpensive digital answering machine. This replaces an ongoing monthly bill with a one-time expense.

➤ If you have a cell phone, cancel your hardline phone.

➤ Cancel cable or satellite TV. Watching television is unproductive and anti-social. Instead of watching TV, go for a walk or invite some friends over.

➤ Cancel your health club membership. You don't have to use a treadmill or stair-stepper to get a good workout. Go running or find some real stairs to climb. You can also ride your bicycle, go hiking, do push-ups and chin-ups, or play basketball.

Conclusion

If we control our expenses, we can decrease our dependence on our salaries. Then, if we get a raise, our savings will experience percentage increases many times greater than the percentage of our raise.

—ɯ—

CHAPTER 9

Save 50 Percent of Your Salary

—ɯ—

If you save 50 percent of your salary, for every month you work, you will save enough to take a month off—*without changing your lifestyle.*

What? Am I crazy? How can you save 50 percent of your salary if you can barely make ends meet?

OK. Maybe 50 percent is too much.

If you save 33 percent of your salary, for every two months you work, you will save enough to take a month off—*without changing your lifestyle.*

What? Am I crazy? How can you save 33 percent of your salary if you can barely make ends meet?

OK. Maybe 33 percent is too much.

If you save 25 percent of your salary, for every three months you work, you will save enough to take a month off—*without changing your lifestyle.*

What? Am I crazy? How can you save 25 percent of your salary if you can barely make ends meet?

I think you get the idea. If your monthly expenses are $2000, every $2000 you save allows you to take a month off *without changing your lifestyle.*

Sometimes we have to take time off because of circumstances beyond our control; the economy goes sour, our company goes out of business, or our jobs are shipped overseas. Having money in the bank can help cushion these hard times and instead of suffering through them, we can use the time to find and create new opportunities in our lives.

EXAMPLE

Since my hellish year of getting out of debt, I have had two other periods of financial hardship.

In both cases, if I didn't have money in the bank and control over my finances, I wouldn't have survived financially. But because I had already created and implemented my money philosophy, I was able to weather both storms.

In late 1999, I was laid off from a contract engineering job in Nashville, Tennessee. Because of the 2000 stock market crash and its devastating effect on the job market, I was out of work for over a year.

I returned to Seattle and decided to go back to school. I paid school costs and living expenses from my own pocket for 11 months. I was able to do so because I had ample savings and minimal expenses.

I went back to work in January of 2001. Then the attacks of 9/11 devastated the aerospace industry. I was laid off in early 2002 and was without a job for a year. I took advantage of the time to write a 231-page novel. Again, my lifestyle didn't change because I had money in the bank and minimal expenses.

Have you ever asked yourself how people who immigrate to the United States can come here, get a low-paying job, and open their own business five years later? How can they do that, making around minimum wage, when you can't, making more than minimum wage?

They save. They save 50 percent or more of their salary. They don't go into debt, they work hard and make other sacrifices, so they can buy their own business and control their financial destinies. They know that by giving up luxuries and "status" now, they will gain luxuries and "status" in the future. They don't buy income-consuming assets, they want to buy income-producing assets.

A financial attitude, based on savings and thrift, used to be commonplace in the United States, but lately, easy credit has enslaved us to our jobs.

Your long-term goal should be to save 25 percent, 33 percent or even 50 percent of your net income, and that doesn't include maxing out your 401k every year (which you should be doing).

How can you save 50 percent of your salary? Is it possible?

The way you look at money has been changing as you read this book. Hopefully, you will no longer embrace debt or waste your money on unnecessary possessions or expenses.

The next chapter will walk you through a nuts-and-bolts method for planning your finances. Once you have a visual representation of your monthly finances, you will see what you have to do to eliminate your debt and maximize your savings. Let's move on and learn concrete methods for incorporating these lessons into our financial lives.

—m—

CHAPTER 10

Control Your Money or Your Money Will Control You

(How to Plan Your Finances)

—ᨓ—

So far, we've learned that:

➤ Debt is slavery.

➤ Money is time.

➤ Possessions are a prison.

➤ The Giant Marketing Machine (GMM) is constantly trying to separate you from your money.

➤ Money buys freedom, options, and opportunity.

➤ You need to control your expenses.

We can extrapolate these points to the following conclusion:

➤ If you don't control your money, your money will control you.

So how can we control our money?

We must *plan our finances*.

To me, "financial planning" is figuring out how much money I make and where my money is going. Most people have no idea how much money is coming in and how much money they spend.

Once you start your financial plan and are face-to-face with the financial realities of your life, it will become clear what you will have to do and change. Most importantly, reading this book to this point should have altered your attitude towards money and you should want to change.

Planning Your Finances Leads to Financial Security

The term "financial security" means different things to different people. To me, being financially secure doesn't mean being independently wealthy; not having to work; having servants bring me martinis by the pool; and flying my private jet to Monaco to party with heiresses, super-models, and rock stars. (Although my method can, if properly applied, eventually lead to being independently wealthy.)

I define "financial security" as:

➤ Being debt-free.

➤ Being in control of my expenses.

➤ Consistently increasing my savings/assets on a monthly basis.

➤ Not being forced to work at a job I dislike just to pay the bills.

The steps towards gaining financial security are:

➤ Planning your finances.

➤ Eliminating your debt.

➤ Minimizing your monthly expenses.

➤ Maximizing your savings.

➤ Maximizing your passive income (from income-producing assets).

We've already talked about minimizing our monthly expenses (Chapter 8), maximizing our savings (Chapter 9), and maximizing our income-generating assets (Chapter 7) and we'll talk in depth about planning our finances later in this chapter. So let's talk about eliminating debt.

Eliminating Debt

How can you eliminate your debt?

➤ Don't accrue more debt.

➤ Remove the temptation by destroying your credit cards. If destroying your credit cards is too drastic for you, you can start with something easier:

+ Leave your credit cards at home.

+ Cancel your cards that have no balance.

+ Change your attitude toward debt. Every time you use credit for a purchase think "Debt is slavery; I am making myself a slave."

➤ Eliminate your debt from the smallest balance to the largest, so you can reward yourself psychologically.

➤ Cancel your credit card accounts as soon as you eliminate the balance.

It is a good idea to keep one credit card account open for emergency purposes. This credit card should be a universally accepted card, such as a Visa.

So are you ready to create your financial plan?

Let's get started!

Creating Your Financial Plan

Here are the steps for creating a successful financial plan:

Step 1: Collect the necessary tools.

Step 2: Figure out how much money you make.

Step 3: Figure out how much money you owe.

Step 4: List your monthly bills.

Step 5: Create a paycheck-by-paycheck financial plan.

Let's walk through a step-by-step example of how I would help somebody plan their finances, minimize their expenses, and eliminate their debt.

For this example, I'm going to use the finances of a single, 25-to-35-year-old, who owns a small condominium, and is paid twice a month.

As you read through the example, think of how you can customize it for your personal situation.

➤ Are you married? What extra expenses are associated with being married?

➤ Do you have kids? What extra expenses come with parenthood?

➤ What about pets? What kind of pet-related expenses do you have?

➤ Do you have job-related expenses?

➤ What other expenses do you have?

✦ Lawn care

✦ House-keeping

✦ Burglar alarm fees

✦ Club membership dues

✦ Taxes

✦ Tuition

✦ Insurance

Step 1: Collect the Necessary Tools

There are several software packages that can help organize your finances. The companies that produce this software try to convince you that money is a complicated subject and you need their software to make sense of it all. Of course, if you don't have a computer, you would have to buy one before you can run the software. You may have to borrow money to buy the computer. That is obviously the wrong way to start your financial plan and eliminate your debt.

Although a computer can be a useful tool for starting a financial and debt-elimination plan, it can detach you from the actions required to be successful. I like getting into the trenches and working directly with the numbers. It's how I developed an instinctive feel for the inflow and outflow of money in my life. The best way to learn how to do something is to actually do it.

My method of financial planning requires only a few tools. These tools are inexpensive and available in most drug stores. In total, they should not cost more than $20.

1) A pen or pencil

   I think it's a safe bet that you probably already have a few of these lying around. If not, buy one. I prefer a pencil because it's easier to make corrections and changes.

2) A spiral notebook

   I started off using a legal pad but prefer a spiral notebook because it keeps everything in order and in one place.

3) A calendar

   You will need a calendar to figure out your paydays for the next six months.

4) A calculator

This is optional, depending on how good you are with arithmetic. My plan requires nothing beyond simple addition and subtraction. A calculator will help guarantee accuracy. You won't need a fancy one.

Step 2: Figure Out How Much Money You Make

Do you know how much money you actually make?

People commonly overestimate their salaries by making some simple mistakes. The most common mistake is that they don't account for the difference between their "gross income" and "net income".

> **Gross income:** *The amount you are paid before federal income taxes, social security taxes, Medicare taxes, state income taxes, etc. This is "pre-tax" income.*

> **Net income:** *How much you receive after all taxes are withheld. This is the amount you have to spend or save. This is "after-tax" income.*

Here's how most people would calculate their monthly income:

EXAMPLE

Your salary is $36,000 per year.

$36,000 divided by 12 months is $3,000.

Therefore, you make $3,000/month.

Technically, this answer is right—if you are calculating your gross income. For our purposes, it is 100 percent wrong. If you think you make $3,000/month, you will create spending habits for $3,000/month.

People usually forget that state and federal governments take large bites out of their paychecks.

These taxes include:

➤ Federal income tax.

➤ State income tax.

➤ OASDI (Old Age, Survivors, and Disability Insurance). This is the official name for Social Security.

➤ Medicare.

If your salary is $36,000 a year, you never see $3,000 a month. After taxes, your take-home—or net pay—is probably around $2,250.

Net income is what we will use in our financial plan.

Q: So how do you figure out your net income?

A: Look at your latest pay-stub (without overtime). How much is the check for? That's how much you make per paycheck.

Step 3: Figure Out How Much Money You Owe

This is the scary step. When I was in financial trouble, I dreaded doing this step. I had no idea how much I owed and I really didn't want to know. When I finally gathered the courage to add up my debts, the figure shocked me. But at least I knew where I stood. I was then able to move forward and create a plan to eliminate my debt and create financial security.

Gather the following bills:

➤ Credit cards

✦ Visa

✦ MasterCard

✦ Discover

✦ Department Store Cards

✦ Gas Cards

➤ Car Loans

➤ Boat Loans

➤ Home Equity Loans

➤ Student Loans

➤ Consumer Loans

On page 1 of your spiral notebook, list all of your debts. Add them up. You should end up with a list that looks something like this:

Debt	
Citibank Visa	$1,800
Nordstrom	$850
Sears	$600
NW Airlines Visa	$2,100
Car	$13,250
Boat	$6,500
Home Equity Loan	$11,500
Student Loan	$4,300
Furniture Loan	$825
Grand Total:	$41,725

Figure 10-1

Holy cow! You never realized you owed that much money, did you? (Note: I didn't include the mortgage because I didn't want you keeling over from shock.)

Now ask yourself, as you look at the size of your debt: Was running up that much debt worth giving up your freedom and becoming a debt slave?

Step 4: List Your Monthly Bills

Collect all of your monthly bill statements. These will include, but are not limited to:

➤ Rent/mortgage

➤ Utilities (electricity, natural gas, water/sewer/garbage, cable TV, phone)

➤ Credit card and other unsecured loan payments

➤ Car, boat, and RV payments

➤ Student loan payments

➤ Cell phone service

➤ Internet service

➤ Insurance premiums (car, renter's, homeowner's)

On page 2 of your notebook, write down the name of the bill and the amount. Use minimum required payments for credit cards. Also, write down the due date and figure out which paycheck the bill will come out of.

Monthly Bills			
Bill	Amount	Due	Check
Mortgage	$725	1st	Check #2
Electricity	$30	1st	Check #2
Natural Gas	$15	15th	Check #1
Water/Sewer/Garbage	$50	15th	Check #1
Cable TV	$40	10th	Check #2
Citibank Visa	$72	15th	Check #1
Nordstrom	$34	1st	Check #2
Sears	$24	1st	Check #2
NW Airlines Visa	$84	20th	Check #1
Car	$275	1st	Check #2
Boat	$90	1st	Check #2
Home Equity Loan	$98	1st	Check #2
Student Loan	$40	15th	Check #1
Furniture Loan	$25	15th	Check #1
Cell Phone	$50	30th	Check #1
Internet	$35	30th	Check #1
Car Insurance	$70	15th	Check #1
Grand Total	$1,757		

Figure 10-2

Step 5: Create a Paycheck-by-Paycheck Financial Plan

Now we're ready to start your paycheck-by-paycheck financial plan. We will assume that you get paid twice a month, on the 1st and the 15th, and bring home $2,250 a month (two $1,125 checks a month). We will use one page per month, two paychecks per page.

Starting on page 3 of your spiral notebook, write the month and year at the top of the page. Then, on the upper left of the page, directly below the month, write "1st Check" and the date of the check. Halfway down the page on the left side, write "2nd Check" and the date of that check. It should look something like this:

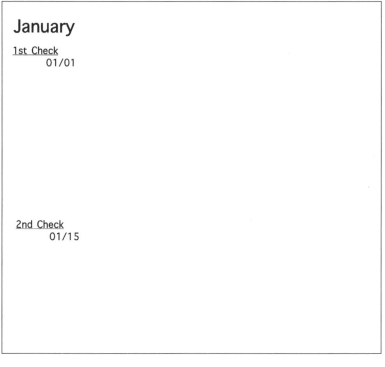

Figure 10-3

Next, write down the check amount, and list the bills that you will be paying with that check in a column. Put check boxes to the left of each bill.

It should look something like this:

January

1st Check		Check Amount	1125.00
01/01	☐	Natural Gas	-15.00
	☐	Water/Sewer/Garbage	-50.00
	☐	Citibank Visa	-72.00
	☐	NW Airlines Visa	-84.00
	☐	Student Loan	-40.00
	☐	Furniture Loan	-25.00
	☐	Cell Phone	-50.00
	☐	Internet Service	-35.00
	☐	Car Insurance	-70.00
		Surplus	684.00
2nd Check		Check Amount	1125.00
01/15	☐	Mortgage	-725.00
	☐	Electricity	-30.00
	☐	Cable	-40.00
	☐	Nordstrom	-34.00
	☐	Sears	-24.00
	☐	Car Payment	-275.00
	☐	Boat Payment	-90.00
	☐	Home Equity Loan	-98.00
		⇨ Surplus	-191.00

Figure 10-4

You can see that you're in trouble on check #2. Your check isn't big enough to cover all your bills. However, you have a surplus on Check #1 that will more than cover the deficit.

Let's jockey around your bills so you end up with a positive surplus for each check. We'll move the car and boat payments from Check #2 to Check #1.

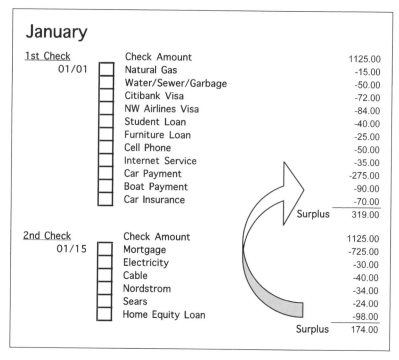

Figure 10-5

Well, it looks like you're in pretty good shape. You have $493 ($319+$174) left over after paying all your bills.

But wait a minute. What about incidentals? What about groceries, gas, shampoo, and entertainment?

The way that I handle miscellaneous expenses is by subtracting a fixed weekly amount in spending cash. The amount will depend on you. You will have to fine-tune the amount.

For now, let's take out $100 per week for miscellaneous expenses.

When you get paid, take out $200 at the ATM. Put one week's worth of cash ($100) in your wallet at a time. Don't keep track of what you spend this money on. You will be able to see the money leave your wallet and have a visual indication of how much money you're spending on incidentals.

If you run out of spending money early, either:

➤ Rein in your spending, or

➤ Increase your weekly allowance.

If you have some left over, either:

➤ Set the money aside for future spending, or

➤ Lower your weekly allowance.

Here's what your financial plan looks like now:

January

1st Check			
01/01	Check Amount		1125.00
	Spending Money (Week #1)		-100.00 ⎱
	Spending Money (Week #2)		-100.00 ⎰
	Natural Gas		-15.00
	Water/Sewer/Garbage		-50.00
	Citibank Visa		-72.00
	NW Airlines Visa		-84.00
	Student Loan		-40.00
	Furniture Loan		-25.00
	Cell Phone		-50.00
	Internet Service		-35.00
	Car Payment		-275.00
	Boat Payment		-90.00
	Car Insurance		-70.00
		Surplus	119.00

2nd Check			
01/15	Check Amount		1125.00
	Spending Money (Week #1)		-100.00 ⎱
	Spending Money (Week #2)		-100.00 ⎰
	Mortgage		-725.00
	Electricity		-30.00
	Cable		-40.00
	Nordstrom		-34.00
	Sears		-24.00
	Home Equity Loan		-98.00
		Surplus	-26.00

Figure 10-6

Whoops! We have a negative "surplus" again on Check #2, so let's move the $30 Electricity bill to Check #1.

Now your financial plan looks like this:

January

1st Check		Check Amount	1125.00
01/01	☐	Spending Money (Week #1)	-100.00
	☐	Spending Money (Week #2)	-100.00
	☐	Natural Gas	-15.00
	☐	Water/Sewer/Garbage	-50.00
	☐	Citibank Visa	-72.00
	☐	NW Airlines Visa	-84.00
	☐	Student Loan	-40.00
	☐	Furniture Loan	-25.00
	☐	Cell Phone	-50.00
	☐	Internet Service	-35.00
	☐	Electricity	-30.00
	☐	Car Payment	-275.00
	☐	Boat Payment	-90.00
	☐	Car Insurance	-70.00
		Surplus	**89.00**
2nd Check		Check Amount	1125.00
01/15	☐	Spending Money (Week #1)	-100.00
	☐	Spending Money (Week #2)	-100.00
	☐	Mortgage	-725.00
	☐	Cable	-40.00
	☐	Nordstrom	-34.00
	☐	Sears	-24.00
	☐	Home Equity Loan	-98.00
		Surplus	**4.00**

Figure 10-7

OK. There is $93 ($89 + $4) left over every month. That's not a lot, but it's a start.

We'll use that surplus to pay down some credit cards, but before we do that, let's look at your expenses.

Minimizing Your Expenses

Now that we have a month's worth of your finances on paper, let's examine it. Is there any way we can minimize your expenses?

Most of the bills are necessities such as electricity, natural gas, and water/sewer/garbage. We can't get rid of these. The same with credit card debt; there's no quick way to get rid of that either. (We'll look at how to eliminate credit card debt later.) Here are a few suggestions to eliminate some monthly bills:

Bill	Monthly Savings
Cancel cable TV	$40.00
Sell the boat, pay off the loan	$90.00
Sell your car, pay off the loan and buy a cheaper car	$275.00
Minimize your miscellaneous expenses	?

Figure 10-8

We actually don't have a lot of choices. Most of the monthly bills are debt payments.

Let's cancel your cable TV for a monthly savings of $40.

Starting Your Debt-Elimination Plan

Once you get a look at where your finances stand, you can make decisions on how to eliminate debt.

Remember that there are two kinds of debt: secured and unsecured.

The easiest debt to eliminate is secured debt. Examples of secured debt includes car loans, mortgages, boat loans, RV loans, etc.

If you owe less than the underlying asset is worth, you can sell the asset and pay off the loan.

How about selling your car?

"But I love my BMW!"

Sure you do. And your BMW is what's keeping you a debt slave. You have to decide whether you love your BMW more than your freedom and peace of mind. If you love your BMW more, you may want to re-examine your priorities.

You can also sell the house and pay off the mortgage.

"But I have to live somewhere! If I sell my house, I'll still have to pay rent."

That's true, but when you rent, you're not responsible for any of the maintenance required with owning a house. Owning a house includes a lot of unexpected expenses. Renting a house doesn't, because if the refrigerator or hot-water heater breaks, your landlord pays the repair bill. Your monthly cost for a rental is fixed.

OK. You don't want to sell the car or the house.

Let's sell the boat.

"But I love my boat!"

Sure you do. Again, you love it so much that you've made yourself a debt slave. Let's get your financial house in order, then you can buy another boat, but this time, pay cash for it.

You owe $6,500 on the boat. The boat is worth $9,000. Let's sell the boat and pay off the loan. You just got rid of $90 in monthly expenses and you have an extra $2,500 ($9,000 – $6,500).

Paying Off Credit Card Debt

Some people suggest first paying off the credit cards with the highest interest rates. I disagree. I suggest you first pay off the credit cards with the smallest balances. There is a psychological reward when you pay off a credit card—it feels good. You can pay off the small-balance cards quickly and the resultant feeling of success and triumph will carry you to your next, larger success.

The important thing to remember is: You must cancel your credit cards as you pay them off. Too many people pay off their credit cards and immediately run them up again. (It is still a good idea to keep one credit card for emergencies. For this example, we'll keep the NW Airlines Visa.)

In our example, we'll start with the Sears card.

OK. Let's take the extra $2,500 you received from selling the boat and pay off your $600 Sears balance, your $850 Nordstrom balance and your $825 furniture loan (since those are your three smallest balances). Make sure you *cancel your Sears and Nordstrom credit cards after they're paid off.*

Your debt table now looks like this:

Debt	
Citibank Visa	$1,800
Nordstrom	$0
Sears	$0
NW Airlines Visa	$2,100
Car	$13,250
Boat	$0
Home Equity Loan	$11,500
Student Loan	$4,300
Furniture Loan	$0
Grand Total:	$32,950

Figure 10-9

Let's eliminate the columns with a zero balance:

Debt	
Citibank Visa	$1,800
NW Airlines Visa	$2,100
Car	$13,250
Home Equity Loan	$11,500
Student Loan	$4,300
Grand Total:	$32,950

Figure 10-10

We'll eliminate the Nordstrom, Sears, boat loan, and furniture loan payments from your January financial plan. It should now look like this:

105

January

1st Check			
01/01	☐	Check Amount	1125.00
	☐	Spending Money (Week #1)	-100.00
	☐	Spending Money (Week #2)	-100.00
	☐	Natural Gas	-15.00
	☐	Water/Sewer/Garbage	-50.00
	☐	Citibank Visa	-72.00
	☐	NW Airlines Visa	-84.00
	☐	Student Loan	-40.00
	☐	Cell Phone	-50.00
	☐	Internet Service	-35.00
	☐	Electricity	-30.00
	☐	Car Payment	-275.00
	☐	Car Insurance	-70.00
		Surplus	204.00

2nd Check			
01/15	☐	Check Amount	1125.00
	☐	Spending Money (Week #1)	-100.00
	☐	Spending Money (Week #2)	-100.00
	☐	Mortgage	-725.00
	☐	Home Equity Loan	-98.00
		Surplus	102.00

Figure 10-11

You now have a surplus of $306 ($204 + $102) every month. We've eliminated five bills (the boat payment, cable TV, Sears, Nordstrom, and the furniture loan) and $213 in monthly financial obligations.

Looking good!

We'll apply the $306 surplus towards your Citibank Visa.

Let's write the outstanding balances of your Citibank Visa and other debt on your spreadsheet (see Figure 10-12). I sorted the rows so the debt is listed together, in ascending order of the outstanding balance. We'll also check off the bills we've paid.

January

			Balance
1st Check	Check Amount	1125.00	
01/01 [x]	Spending Money (Week #1)	-100.00	
[x]	Spending Money (Week #2)	-100.00	
[x]	Natural Gas	-15.00	
[ ]	Water/Sewer/Garbage	-50.00	
[x]	Cell Phone	-50.00	
[ ]	Internet Service	-35.00	
[ ]	Electricity	-30.00	
[x]	Citibank Visa	-276.00	1524.00
[ ]	NW Airlines Visa	-84.00	2100.00
[ ]	Student Loan	-40.00	4300.00
[ ]	Car Payment	-275.00	13250.00
[x]	Car Insurance	-70.00	
	Surplus	0.00	
2nd Check	Check Amount	1125.00	
10- [ ]	Spending Money (Week #1)	-100.00	
[ ]	Spending Money (Week #2)	-100.00	
[ ]	Citibank Visa	-102.00	1422.00
[ ]	Home Equity Loan	-98.00	11500.00
[ ]	Mortgage	-725.00	140000.00
	Surplus	0.00	

Figure 10-12

Do you see how we now have a snapshot of our monthly finances? We can actually see how much money is coming in, how much is going out, and how much debt is being paid off. So let's plan February.

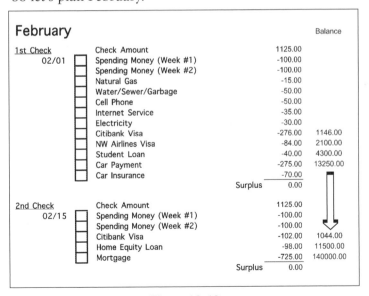

February

			Balance
1st Check	Check Amount	1125.00	
02/01 [ ]	Spending Money (Week #1)	-100.00	
[ ]	Spending Money (Week #2)	-100.00	
[ ]	Natural Gas	-15.00	
[ ]	Water/Sewer/Garbage	-50.00	
[ ]	Cell Phone	-50.00	
[ ]	Internet Service	-35.00	
[ ]	Electricity	-30.00	
[ ]	Citibank Visa	-276.00	1146.00
[ ]	NW Airlines Visa	-84.00	2100.00
[ ]	Student Loan	-40.00	4300.00
[ ]	Car Payment	-275.00	13250.00
[ ]	Car Insurance	-70.00	
	Surplus	0.00	
2nd Check	Check Amount	1125.00	
02/15 [ ]	Spending Money (Week #1)	-100.00	
[ ]	Spending Money (Week #2)	-100.00	
[ ]	Citibank Visa	-102.00	1044.00
[ ]	Home Equity Loan	-98.00	11500.00
[ ]	Mortgage	-725.00	140000.00
	Surplus	0.00	

Figure 10-13

By the end of February, your Citibank Visa balance is down to $1,044. Do you now see how money is time? Since you're paying $378 per month ($276 + $102) towards your Citibank Visa balance, it's going to take three more months to pay it off.

Debt is slavery.

Unexpected or Unusual Expenses

If any unexpected or unusual expenses come up, you can add a row to your monthly financial plan to account for the expense. This will also work if you want to buy some clothes or save money for a trip.

We'll add $50 for a Valentine's Day gift and start saving $50 per paycheck for a trip to Mexico. We'll keep a running count of how much we've saved for the Mexico trip in the "Balance" column.

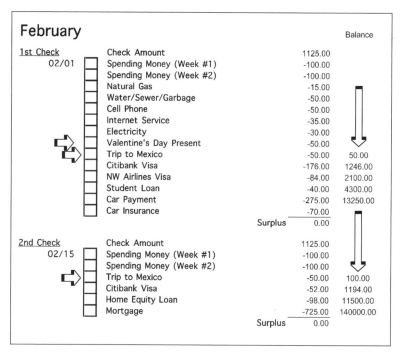

February		Balance
1st Check		
02/01 — Check Amount	1125.00	
Spending Money (Week #1)	-100.00	
Spending Money (Week #2)	-100.00	
Natural Gas	-15.00	
Water/Sewer/Garbage	-50.00	
Cell Phone	-50.00	
Internet Service	-35.00	
Electricity	-30.00	
Valentine's Day Present	-50.00	
Trip to Mexico	-50.00	50.00
Citibank Visa	-176.00	1246.00
NW Airlines Visa	-84.00	2100.00
Student Loan	-40.00	4300.00
Car Payment	-275.00	13250.00
Car Insurance	-70.00	
Surplus	0.00	
2nd Check		
02/15 — Check Amount	1125.00	
Spending Money (Week #1)	-100.00	
Spending Money (Week #2)	-100.00	
Trip to Mexico	-50.00	100.00
Citibank Visa	-52.00	1194.00
Home Equity Loan	-98.00	11500.00
Mortgage	-725.00	140000.00
Surplus	0.00	

Figure 10-14

Note that by adding the extra Valentine's Day expense and the Mexico trip, we are not paying off our debts as quickly as before. This is a personal decision you have to make regarding your priorities. That's OK as long as you plan for it.

Create a False Sense of Scarcity

There's another idea I'd like to introduce regarding your financial plan. At some point in time, you will have a lot of excess money at the end of the month. You may be tempted to spend it unwisely.

I suggest you do what I do: Create a "false sense of scarcity."

Let's take a look at October's financial plan. It shows the same person as before, but with no debt except their mortgage, which means there's a $875 surplus each month:

```
October                                              Balance

1st Check        Check Amount              1125.00
    10/01    ☐   Spending Money (Week #1)  -100.00
             ☐   Spending Money (Week #2)  -100.00
             ☐   Natural Gas                -15.00
             ☐   Water/Sewer/Garbage        -50.00
             ☐   Cell Phone                 -50.00
             ☐   Internet Service           -35.00
             ☐   Electricity                -30.00
             ☐   Car Insurance              -70.00
                              Surplus       675.00

2nd Check        Check Amount              1125.00
    10/15    ☐   Spending Money (Week #1)  -100.00
             ☐   Spending Money (Week #2)  -100.00
             ☐   Mortgage                  -725.00   140000.00
                              Surplus       200.00
```

Figure 10-15

If we let the surplus build up, the temptation increases to spend it on something stupid. To combat that temptation, let's create a monthly "expense" called "Savings."

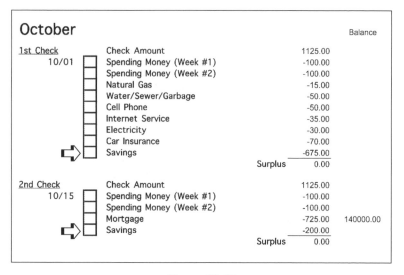

Figure 10-16

Because we're "paying" our savings account $875 per month, we've created a "sense of scarcity"—we have extra money every month, but we don't feel like it. The surplus money isn't easily accessible for irrational spending. We are also creating an income-producing asset—savings.

Conclusion

I think you have a feel for how it's done. So try it with your own finances.

When you see how much money comes in and out of your life, and where it's going, you can begin to control your finances. Soon, you will build a sense of confidence, that *you* are in control of your financial destiny.

It can change your life.

Good luck!

CHAPTER 11

A Bonus

—ᴗ—

So now you have the knowledge and tools to gain control of your financial life. However, once you figure out the extent of your debt, you may feel overwhelmed and wonder why someone didn't teach you this stuff years ago.

All of us occasionally think, "I wish I had done that when I was younger," or "I wish I was X years old again," or "If I only knew then what I know now."

Unfortunately, it's a fantasy and isn't going to happen.

We all fall into the "woulda, coulda, shoulda" trap, which never gets us anywhere but in the dumps.

One day, while wallowing in "woulda, coulda, shouldas", I realized something—another life truth:

You will never be younger than you are at this moment.

If we concentrate on this moment, on what opportunities we have *now*, and what we can do *now*, we can minimize our regrets in the future.

So take what you've learned from this book and apply it. Teach it to your children. Gain control of your life and free yourself from the shackles of debt.

Do it now.

And the next time you find yourself wallowing in "woulda, coulda, shouldas", remember:

You will never be younger than you are at this moment.

Then get to work!

—ɯ—

Appendix

—∿∿—

Here are some explanations for terms and concepts I use in this book.

Amortization

"Amortizing" a loan means calculating monthly payments, including the loan's interest rate, over the length of a loan.

For example, the monthly payment for a $100 loan amortized over 10 months at 0% is $10 ($100 divided by 10 months = $10).

When the same $100 loan is amortized over 20 months at 0%, the monthly payment is $5 ($100 divided by 20 months is $5).

I used an interest rate of 0% to simplify these calculations. When the interest rate is not 0%, the calculations are a little more complicated and it's easiest to use one of the many loan calculators available on the internet to calculate loan payments.

Collateral

Collateral is property that is accepted as security for a loan.

For example, the collateral for a car loan is the car itself. If you stop making your car loan payments, the bank can seize the car from you and sell it to get its money back.

Equity

Equity is the portion of an asset that you own.

For example, if you own a car that is worth $10,000 and you owe $6,000 on it, your equity is $4,000 ($10,000 minus $6,000).

Similarly, if you own a house that is worth $200,000 and you owe $120,000 on it, your equity is $80,000 ($200,000 minus $120,000).

It's nice to have equity, but it's not the same as having money in the bank. Unlike money in a savings account, you cannot spend equity unless you borrow against it.

Let's use the house example above to illustrate this point. Your home equity is $80,000. Let's say you want to use $10,000 to pay for a new roof.

The only way to extract $10,000 from your home equity is to borrow the money, using your home as collateral.

The two most common methods to borrow money against your home equity are:

➤ Taking out a home equity loan, which is a second loan that, like your mortgage, uses your house as collateral.

➤ Refinancing your mortgage and extracting some of your equity as cash. However, remember that extracting equity from your mortgage also increases the outstanding loan balance by the amount you extract.

Interest

Interest is the "fee" lenders charge when they loan money. It is calculated as a percentage of the outstanding loan balance.

Interest rates are usually presented as an "annual rate". However, just because it's called an "annual rate" doesn't mean it is calculated only once a year. Interest can be calculated daily, weekly, monthly, or quarterly.

To illustrate how interest works, suppose I asked you to lend me $10 today and promised to pay you back in 30 days.

Would you do it?

It would probably depend on how well you know and trust me. If I had a reputation for dishonesty, I doubt you would lend me the money. However, if I was your best friend and the most honest guy you knew, you'd probably lend me the money.

Now suppose you are a bank. Banks don't personally know everybody who comes in to borrow money. When the bank lends money to someone, there's a risk that the money will not be paid back. Also, banks must make a profit to stay in business.

To make up for the risk and to make a profit, lenders charge interest.

When you fill out a loan application, the bank uses your information to calculate their risk in loaning you money.

If you have a bad credit history, the bank will see you as a high risk (to not pay back the loan). They will either decline your loan application or charge a higher interest rate to compensate for the chance that you may not pay back their money.

On the other hand, if you have a stellar credit history, you are a low risk and banks will fall over each other trying to loan you money (at lower interest rates) because they know you are highly likely to pay back the loan.

Loan risk is also affected by the length of the loan. For example, there is more risk loaning money over long periods of time, so long-term loans will generally have higher interest rates than short-term loans to compensate for the greater risk.

Mortgage

Mortgages are loans used to buy real estate. The most common repayment periods are 15 and 30 years. There are several types of residential mortgages.

Fixed-Rate Mortgages

For fixed-rate mortgages, the interest rate remains the same for the entire length of the loan. The interest rate is based on market-determined long-term interest rates (in contrast to Adjustable-Rate Mortgages, which are based on short-term interest rates). Since the interest rate is fixed, the payment will also remain the same over the life of the loan.

For example, a 30-year, $100,000 mortgage at 6% will have a monthly payment of $599. It's the same payment, every month, for 30 years.

Mortgage Amount	Interest Rate	Length of Mortgage	Monthly Payment
15 Year Mortgage			
$100,000.00	6.00%	15 Years	$843.00
$100,000.00	7.00%	15 Years	$898.00
$100,000.00	8.00%	15 Years	$955.00
$100,000.00	9.00%	15 Years	$1,014.00
30 Year Mortgage			
$100,000.00	6.00%	30 Years	$599.00
$100,000.00	7.00%	30 Years	$665.00
$100,000.00	8.00%	30 Years	$733.00
$100,000.00	9.00%	30 Years	$804.00

Figure A-1
Monthly Payments for Fixed-Rate Mortgages

As you can see, higher interest rates mean higher monthly payments. Also, a shorter mortgage length means higher monthly payments (since you're paying back the loan more quickly).

Adjustable-Rate Mortgages (ARMs)

As you can probably guess from the name, the interest rate for an Adjustable-Rate Mortgage does not remain fixed, but can adjust over the life of the loan, which also means that the payments may change over the life of the loan.

The interest rate for ARMs is based on short-term interest rates (in contrast to Fixed-Rate Mortgages, which are based on long-term interest rates).

Adjustable-rate mortgages are available in different lengths. The interest rate is fixed for a period of time, after which the rate may be adjusted. There are usually caps on how much the interest rates can be adjusted per adjustment period and over the life of the loan (see Figure A-2).

Type of ARM	Initial Interest Rate	Cap Per Adjustment Period	Lifetime Cap	Description
3/1	5.00%	2.00%	6.00%	The interest rate remains fixed at 5.00% for 3 years (the 3 in "3/1"), after which it may be adjusted every year (the 1 in "3/1") a maximum of 2.00%. The maximum adjustment over the life of the loan is 6.00%, so you will never pay more than 11% interest.
5/1	5.00%	1.00%	8.00%	The interest rate remains fixed at 5.00% for 5 years, after which it may be adjusted every year a maximum of 1.00%. The maximum adjustment over the life of the loan is 8.00%, so you will never pay more than 13% interest.

Figure A-2
Examples of ARM Types

Choosing an adjustable-rate mortgage instead of a fixed-rate mortgage can be advantageous if short-term interest rates are a lot lower than long-term interest rates (see "Interest"). If that's the case, the monthly payments for an ARM will be much lower than for a fixed-rate loan.

For example, a $100,000 fixed-rate loan at 6% has a monthly payment of $599. An equivalent ARM may have an interest rate of only 5% and a monthly payment of $536.

The danger of having an ARM is your monthly payment may not remain the same for the length of the loan. If interest rates go up, your payment will probably increase after the "fixed-rate" period is over (see Figure A-3).

Loan Amount	Initial Interest Rate	Initial Monthly Payment	New Interest Rate	New Monthly Payment	% Increase in Monthly Payment
$100,000	5.00%	$536.00	7.00%	$665.00	24.07%

Figure A-3
The Danger of ARMs

On the flip side, if interest rates go down, your payment may be adjusted lower.

Interest-Only Mortgages

Interest-only mortgages have recently become very popular. Payments on an interest-only loan tend to be much lower than payments on a standard loan because your monthly payments only pay the interest on the loan and do not pay down the outstanding balance.

On a standard loan, the monthly payment pays interest and the rest goes toward paying down your loan balance. Over time, the interest portion of your monthly payment decreases, while the portion applied toward the principal increases, until eventually you pay off your loan. (see Figure A-4).

Month	Monthly Payment	Applied Towards Principal	Applied Towards Interest	Total Interest Paid	Loan Balance
1	$86.99	$80.32	$6.67	$6.67	$919.68
2	$86.99	$80.86	$6.13	$12.80	$838.82
3	$86.99	$81.40	$5.59	$18.39	$757.42
4	$86.99	$81.94	$5.05	$23.44	$675.48
5	$86.99	$82.49	$4.50	$27.94	$592.99
6	$86.99	$83.04	$3.95	$31.89	$509.95
7	$86.99	$83.59	$3.40	$35.29	$426.36
8	$86.99	$84.15	$2.84	$38.13	$342.21
9	$86.99	$84.71	$2.28	$40.41	$257.50
10	$86.99	$85.27	$1.72	$42.13	$172.23
11	$86.99	$85.84	$1.15	$43.28	$86.39
12	$86.99	$86.39	$0.58	$43.86	$0.00

Figure A-4
A **standard** 12-month loan at 8.0% for $1,000

Let's compare an interest-only loan (Figure A-5) with the standard loan shown in Figure A-4.

Month	Monthly Payment	Applied Towards Principal	Applied Towards Interest	Total Interest Paid	Loan Balance
1	$6.67	$0.00	$6.67	$6.67	$1,000.00
2	$6.67	$0.00	$6.67	$13.34	$1,000.00
3	$6.67	$0.00	$6.67	$20.01	$1,000.00
4	$6.67	$0.00	$6.67	$26.68	$1,000.00
5	$6.67	$0.00	$6.67	$33.35	$1,000.00
6	$6.67	$0.00	$6.67	$40.02	$1,000.00
7	$6.67	$0.00	$6.67	$46.69	$1,000.00
8	$6.67	$0.00	$6.67	$53.36	$1,000.00
9	$6.67	$0.00	$6.67	$60.03	$1,000.00
10	$6.67	$0.00	$6.67	$66.70	$1,000.00
11	$6.67	$0.00	$6.67	$73.37	$1,000.00
12	$6.67	$0.00	$6.67	$80.04	$1,000.00

Figure A-5
An **interest-only** loan for $1,000 at 8.0% over 12 months

Your monthly payments are a lot lower for the interest-only loan, but even after making 12 payments, you haven't made a dent in the outstanding balance. You still owe $1,000 on the loan.

Now assume it's a $100,000 interest-only mortgage at 8%, amortized over 30 years (360 months).

Month	Payment	Principal	Interest	Total Interest Paid	Loan Balance
1	$666.67	$0.00	$666.67	$666.67	$100,000.00
2	$666.67	$0.00	$666.67	1332.89	$100,000.00
3	$666.67	$0.00	$666.67	1998.66	$100,000.00
4	$666.67	$0.00	$666.67	2663.98	$100,000.00
5	$666.67	$0.00	$666.67	3328.84	$100,000.00
6	$666.67	$0.00	$666.67	3993.24	$100,000.00
7	$666.67	$0.00	$666.67	4657.18	$100,000.00
8	$666.67	$0.00	$666.67	5320.65	$100,000.00
9	$666.67	$0.00	$666.67	5983.65	$100,000.00
10	$666.67	$0.00	$666.67	6646.18	$100,000.00
11	$666.67	$0.00	$666.67	7308.24	$100,000.00
12	$666.67	$0.00	$666.67	7969.82	$100,000.00

Figure A-6
$100,000 interest-only loan at 8.0% amortized for 30 years

You're paying $666.67 a month, yet, in month #12, you're no closer to paying off your loan than you were in month #1. You still owe $100,000 on the mortgage.

Interest-only loans are generally an unwise choice.

Principal

The principal of a loan is the outstanding amount owed on the loan.

About the Author

—๛—

MIKE MIHALIK was born in Tokyo, Japan to an American father and a Japanese mother. Three years later, his family moved to Seattle, Washington. When Mike was 13 years old, his father died, leaving his mother to raise Mike and his sister alone.

Mike was a good student and earned a Bachelor of Science degree in Mechanical Engineering from the University of Washington. During college, Mike ran up huge debts financing his lifestyle. Even after he graduated and began work as an aerospace engineer, Mike's debts exploded out of control.

Mike decided he needed to change how he handled his money. He created a way of thinking about money and planning his finances that freed him from the slavery of debt and allowed him to regain control of his life.

Mike has since refined his philosophy about money. He has created a set of ideas and rules for financial security that can be applied at any income level. Now that he has successfully implemented these ideas in his own life, he wishes to share them with others who may be straining under the burdens of debt.

—๛—

OCTOBER MIST
PUBLISHING

Order Form

Mail Orders: October Mist Publishing
                         PO Box 70809
                         Seattle, WA 98127   USA
                         SAN 850-959X

E-mail Orders: Orders@OctoberMist.com

Fax Orders: 480-393-4647. Complete and fax this form.

Toll-Free Phone Orders: 1-800-748-8390, within the U.S.

Please send the following books:

Title _____Qty _____

Title _____Qty _____

Shipping/Billing Information:

Name _____

Address _____

City _____State _____ Zip _____

Telephone _____

E-mail Address _____

Payment Information:

Method of Payment: ❑ Check   ❑ Discover   ❑ Visa

                              ❑ AMEX   ❑ MasterCard

Card Number _____

Name on Card _____ Exp. Date _____

Sales Tax: Please add 8.8% sales tax for orders shipped to Washington State.

Shipping and Handling (good through December, 2007):

U.S.: $3.95 for the first item and $2.25 for each additional item. All books shipped via U.S. Postal Service Media Mail unless otherwise requested.

International: $9.95 for the first item ($7.95 for Canada and Mexico) and $5.95 for each additional item.

100% Money-Back Guarantee: All products may be returned for a full refund, less shipping and handling, within 30 days of purchase.